John Bates: Fashion Designer

To: Julian,

Best wishes

John Bates.

2012.

John Bates:
Fashion Designer

Richard Lester
Foreword by Marit Allen
ACC Editions

Opposite page
First gear: a dramatic jump suit in
windowpane check, shot by Duffy
for *The Sunday Times* magazine.
Duffy/The Sunday Times

ISBN 9781851495702

British Library Cataloguing-in-Publication Data
A catalogue record for this book is available from the
British Library.

Publication designed and typeset by Northbank, Bath

Printed in China

ACC Editions. An imprint of
Antique Collectors' Club Ltd.,
Woodbridge, Suffolk, IP12 4SD

Contents

Foreword:
Marit Allen

1941-2007

John Bates was a most remarkable player on the scene of British Fashion in the 1960s and '70s. Remarkable because he was the tallest, the most handsome, most self-effacing, shy, and yet self-confident one of a group of young people who changed the image of London.

The wave of creativity stretched across every medium – from film, art, music, literature, architecture, now all well-documented. However, John Bates dropped from the press and museum radar until the show of his work at the Fashion Museum in Bath in 2006, which was attended by 28,000 people, somewhat setting the record straight – which is also what this book aims to do.

He was a major part of the tangible current which ran through fashion and became the wearable manifestation of a cultural revolution, a new freedom from convention and tradition, clothes for the brave new young, literally Ready-to-Wear.

John Bates didn't come through the Royal College of Art, like many of his contemporaries. He learnt the business the hard way, by working in a variety of businesses from couture to wholesale. He didn't have a publicity machine, but what he did have was an unswerving instinct for what was new, modern, cutting edge.

He knew about impact, and textures, and had a real feeling for shapes that would be fun to wear. He mastered the geometry of cut, multiplied by the impact of colour.

His first workroom and showroom was tiny, up narrow, blue-carpeted stairs, down a hidden, hard-to-find short-cut between Bond Street and Oxford Street. Caterine Milinaire and I were editing the 'Young Fashion' pages for *Queen* magazine, in 1963/4, and I well remember the excitement of those first collections, and how difficult it was to encourage John to come out from behind the curtain to be congratulated. His shyness was engaging; his talent, without doubt.

John and I became firm friends. We used to meet on Tuesdays for a toasted cheese and tomato sandwich, as we scanned the jumbled antique market just north of Oxford Street, and scored a painting here, a bedspread there.

We were part of an extraordinary 'Youth Quake' junket, swept up by the entrepreneur Paul Young, to showcase clothes he had bought from the young English designers for his new store Paraphernalia, on Madison Avenue, New York. They were heady

Marit Allen on her wedding day, wearing a metallic silver dress and matching coat designed by John Bates.
John Bates

days and nights, with fashion shows and parties peopled by the glitterati, including Teddy Kennedy. Cameras flashed as Mary Quant, Alexander Plunkett-Green, Sally Tuffin and Marion Foale, Jean Muir, James Wedge, models, movers and shakers rocked the night away in the shortest skirts and hottest pants of the London Hipsters.

By 1966 John was experimenting with new fabrics and daring colours – fluorescent colours, and newly treated synthetics. He used minutely pleated nylon ruffled layers edged with pink threads for a halter-necked confection which barely came to mid-thigh, and fluorescent green nylon dissected by flashes of pink in a brilliant triangle of a dress. Collection after collection, his clothes were irresistible to photograph, and equally irresistible to wear.

John became part of the fabric of my life when he designed and made my wedding dress in 1966, and, undeterred by the fact that there was no practical silver fabric made at the time, he improvised, using what was essentially silvered paper card for the highwayman's collar on the coat and matching polo-neck of the micro gabardine dress beneath. Sounds a little crazy, but the outfit survived to be in the Fashion Museum in Bath in 2006.

By this time, John's work was photographed by all the great photographers of the day, on all the iconic models. On Twiggy by Beaton, Jill Kennington by Helmut Newton, Jean Shrimpton and Penelope Tree by Bailey. And on, and on.

Then came *The Avengers,* speaking of icons. Diana Rigg, in John's fantastic costumes, became a new heroine against whom all other heroines would be measured. The jumpsuit, the catsuit, the hipsters became the fantasy of every watching man, the envy of women everywhere. He gave the series an identity and a style never before seen on British television, and together with Rigg's ironic humour and stylish acting, *The Avengers* became an unprecedented international success.

The volume of John's work grew immensely, and internationally, and the company moved to an elegant, modern workspace in Noel Street, W.1. His work was seen everywhere in magazines and newsprint, and worn everywhere from Ascot to Aberdovey.

John recognized and encouraged the talent in others. He championed Bill Gibb, and secured a design position for him with Monty Black's company, Baccarat, which was to be the start of Bill's meteoric and brilliant career.

John's home was a centre for warm, informal evenings. I remember one such, a Moroccan style affair, with everyone seated on floor cushions, feasting, and laughing uncontrollably with Elaine Stritch, who was the toast of the West End stage at the time, and a great fan of John's clothes.

John Bates came on to the London fashion scene like a bolt of blue light, trailing sparks of excitement, designing the shortest skirts, the swiftest shapes, the surest colours. His clothes were witty, and fun to wear, and he was considerate towards women of all shapes and sizes – generously cutting across convention, so that there was something for everyone to enjoy. His energy was endless, as his sketches show. This assessment of his work is well overdue, and will set the record straight as to his contribution to the looks which were the heartbeat of London in the Sixties.

1964: John Bates in the stockroom of Jean Varon, Woodstock Street, with house model Judith Allera in a banded crepe dress selling at 21 guineas.
Norman Eales/Fashion Museum, Bath

A foothold in the business

1

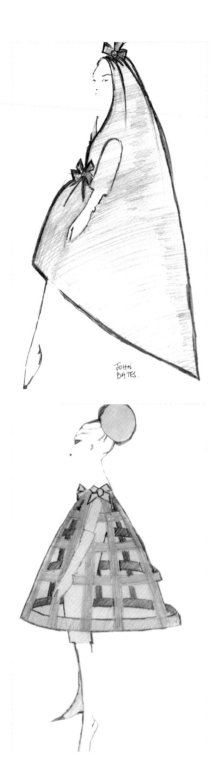

The importance of a strong silhouette: pages from John's 1958 sketchbook.
John Bates

John Bates is remarkably modest when reviewing his career in fashion. 'A part of it is luck; being in the right place at the right time'. Fashion writers and the wearers of his clothes would argue that it is more to do with a prodigious talent for being able to make women look attractive, whatever their budget.

His innovative designs for the label Jean Varon, for Diana Rigg in *The Avengers* and the exquisitely crafted clothes of his own name brand earned him a worldwide reputation and over 300 appearances in the pages of *Vogue* in the twenty years of his mainstream career, but the beginning was tough and success took time in coming.

London in the late 1950s could not have been more different from today's capital of readily available style. Fashion existed strictly on three levels: Couture, adapting looks from Paris, The Boutique, stocking select designers for a middle market clientele, and the all-powerful department store – not just in the major urban centres, but with branches throughout the suburbs and smaller towns. Anyone wanting to make a name in fashion faced the choice of which level to try and crack. For John, with no training and recently out of the army after two years' National Service, the couturier Herbert Sidon of Sloane Street provided the answer.

> 'I started by taking messages, cleaning, being taught to sketch. If the tea needed making I'd make it. If a client came in I could watch how they were dealt with, how they were greeted. As soon as I'd finished that I'd be off down the road again on errands – then I could sit and sketch.'

Sidon admired the French couturiers Givenchy and Balenciaga and the greater part of John's training was to study old fashion magazines and constantly sketch. Simplicity and silhouette was the mantra. 'I was untrained as a cutter, but it was necessary to know where the seams had to go and indicate this on the sketch. If he didn't like a design he'd tear it up. It was good training – but very hard at the time.'

Paid £4 per week, the hours were long but the experience was invaluable as an introduction to the upper end of the London fashion world. In addition to private clients, Herbert Sidon also showed to a middle market wholesale firm which would buy designs from the collection it deemed suitable for adaptation to the wholesale market. Eventually two designs by John were included in the show and both were selected by the firm. With Sidon's blessing John accepted a job offer from the wholesalers which meant both a foothold in a different market and the chance to put his designs into production.

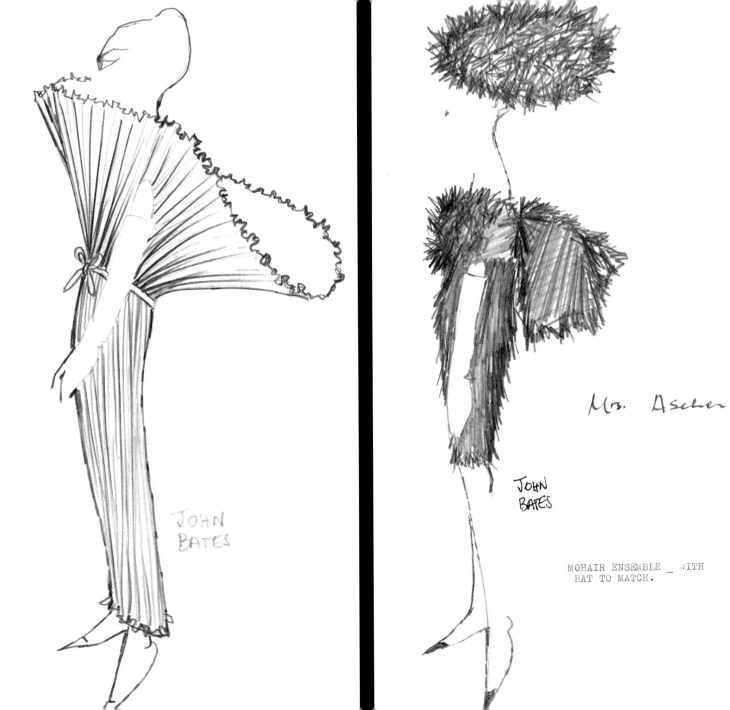

JOHN
BATES

Mrs. Ascher

JOHN
BATES

MOHAIR ENSEMBLE _ WITH
HAT TO MATCH.

Traditional evening dresses provided Jean Varon with a vital source of income in the early 1960s: this example in cerise satin with French lace bodice sold at 23 guineas.
National Magazines

The relief at leaving a job with which he was becoming more disenchanted by the day was short-lived. 'When I arrived for work at the wholesale house, the woman who was head cutter didn't like my sketches, saying they were more suited to *Vogue* magazine than a wholesale company. I found out later that Sidon had telephoned them saying he had second thoughts, and maybe I was not ready yet, and they should continue buying suitable samples from him. I went from earning £4 a week with free accommodation to being unemployed with rent of £4 a week to find – no unemployment benefit in those days. Shy as I was, I forced myself to go knocking on doors trying to sell sketches, walking everywhere because it was a choice of tube fare or loaf of bread. Two people who I shall ever be grateful to are Belinda Bellville, who had also worked for Herbert Sidon, and Mrs Peet, who owned the avant-garde fashion shop Mary Fair off Baker Street. These two kept me going at a very tough time'.

John's next move was to Diana Dresses, a wholesaler in the Edgware Road and supplier to C&A, firmly at the opposing end of the market to Sidon of Sloane Street. There he was expected to design and cut, making a dress out of no more than a yard of sixty-inch-wide fabric, with the minimum of trimming. 'Coming from a designer that had the attitude of couture into a place like that was an eye-opener.'

Through guile, bluff and use of their stock patterns he hung onto the job for three months, but John's luck was about to change through a chance meeting with businessmen Eric West and Bernard Bragg. Both had arrived from Ireland with some money to invest in a fashion business, and their first port of call had been Herbert Sidon. Their first meeting with John had not been auspicious. He, pushed into the room by Sidon to talk to potential investors, was tall, shy, very thin and wearing tight black and white check trousers; the tweed-clad businessmen within seemed unlikely future business partners.

Walking back to his room in Portobello Road from Diana Dresses some months after this first meeting, it was by chance that the two businessmen, now trying to track John down after failing to strike a deal with Sidon, drove by.

'They were looking for one person in London – it was a needle in a haystack. It just so happened that I was crossing Edgware Road and they were driving round a corner. It was luck.'

John agreed to work with the two businessmen, but had unfinished business at Diana Dresses. Demoralised by having to design in less than a yard of fabric, he produced a group of dresses using up to eight yards each, keeping the samples

under wraps until presentation day to the owners. 'The shock on their faces as the models twirled in front of them and they worked out the yardage was gratifying. "And that," I said, "is what I really want to design, and I'm leaving" – probably two seconds before I was sacked.'

And so the business was born in early 1959 – in a first floor flat in Ladbroke Grove. John's first collections were very small and shown to private clients invited to the flat, but things went far from smoothly.

> 'The neighbours complained that the flat was being used for business purposes – so we were thrown out. We moved about four times, each time getting evicted, until we got fed up with people not being able to find us. We decided that Eric and Bernard, not prolific spenders, would have to bite the bullet and invest in a more permanent home for us to work from. There was a small house off Bond Street in Woodstock Street available at £1,200 a year which for us was a huge undertaking.'

The business could not have been better placed geographically at this time in London. The department stores lay to the north and east on Oxford Street and Regent Street. To the south was New Bond Street and to the west the heart of traditional London couture, Mayfair.

That was the beginning of Jean Varon, a name chosen for tactical reasons. 'Jean' is French for 'John' and there was nobody in the rag trade directory under 'V' – to be at the front of these it had to be 'Va'. 'Varon' came along, and it looked good graphically. 'We wanted something very simple and stylish and as the French influence dominated the London fashion scene in the 1950s it seemed to us that we stood a better chance of getting publicity and attracting shop buyers if we at least looked French. Smart shops tended to have French names like Chez Elle and Mademoiselle.'

It was the traditional department store which was to provide the first business for the fledgling company. John designed a small collection and took it on himself to write seven letters a week to editors and buyers in order to get somebody interested in at least looking, until the buyer for the French Room in Fenwick's of Bond Street visited 17 Woodstock Street. 'She couldn't buy what I was showing, it was too different for her customers, but she would sell draped dresses and bridal. We needed to pay the rent, so draped dresses and wedding gowns it had to be! It was difficult to buy really stylish draped dresses so I suppose I filled a gap in the market. You certainly couldn't buy the sort of designs I was producing at the wholesale level – it was too much work'.

To look at those designs now they offer little hint of the radical innovation in shape and textiles that was to establish John's name in the mid 1960s. However it meant the first appearances of the Jean Varon label in the press and the chance to establish the reputation of the firm. One of the most vital contacts was *Flair,* a magazine aimed at a younger reader who could not afford couture or boutique clothes. It was a perfect match for the newly-established label and a chance to promote the shorter, younger look.

> 'Flair magazine was very supportive – they gave Jean Varon pages and covers, which nobody else at the time would do. We did the stockings to match the dresses, which *Flair* magazine photographed. Making the stockings was a nightmare!'

Inevitably it was the wedding dress which gained the first major press credit to Jean Varon. Ernestine Carter, who had been introduced to John's work by Brigid Keenan, her 'Young Ideas' editor, featured a satin crinoline wedding dress in *The Sunday Times* in June 1961. The look was traditional, full skirted, opulent with hand-made fabric roses running the full length of the front. *Harper's Bazaar* carried a Harrods promotion for a 'Younger Set' evening dress by John in pastel pink chiffon, with huge, romantic skirts and a pearlised embroidered bodice. Cocktail dresses were fitted and sleek with just a hint of pleated details or a bow at the waist or collar, a detail which was to be a Jean Varon hallmark in years to come. The puffball skirt also featured in 1961, with the Jean Varon version in tiered striped taffeta. Wedding dresses retailed at twenty-five to thirty-five guineas, cocktails dresses at around fifteen guineas.

Opposite page
June 1961: Ernestine Carter for *The Sunday Times* features a Jean Varon wedding dress with huge fabric roses, 29 guineas from Fenwick's, with gloves by Dents.
Alec Murray/Fashion Museum, Bath

Above Tiers of lace-edged organza and net: a classic Jean Varon wedding dress modelled by Jean Shrimpton, June 1962.
Sandra Lousanda/Fashion Museum, Bath

Left From the 1962 Harrods 'Younger Set' collection, a Jean Varon chiffon evening dress with a shimmer of pearlised embroidery to the bodice.
National Magazines

A constant source of encouragement was Marit Allen at *Queen* magazine. 'She would give me a whole page. It was exciting to get publicity but it was tough to try and flog your designs. After designing a collection I would spend my time trying to get people to come in and see it.'

Even with publicity, selling a collection to the shops meant hours of wasted visits and letter writing. When a shop did agree to take a design it was not uncommon just to take a sample to put in the window as opposed to placing an order. 'Then they'd sell it and you'd be left with nothing – but it would give you an entrée into that shop.'

Traditional boutique and store buyers were formidable in their formality, often staying in the West End for several days around their various appointments with the wholesale firms. 'They'd sweep in like three masted schooners in full sail, fully made-up with hat and gloves, a daunting sight.' The fashion editors were no less imposing, being headed by Ernestine Carter of *The Sunday Times*, Winefrede Jackson of the *Sunday Telegraph* and Alison Settle of *Vogue* – all addressed as Mrs or Miss, never by their christian names unless invited to do so. 'When that day came it was akin to the bestowing of a knighthood.'

'Trying to get buyers into your showroom was like trying to get royalty to visit – that's why the publicity was so important. The day I got a write-up from Ernestine Carter in *The Sunday Times*, they all changed. You didn't get in unless you'd been going for a little while, but you had to prove yourself to her too.'

If the first of John's big breaks was selling to Fenwick's, the second and one of the most important for the business came from Wallis Shops. Although the brand still exists today, its early 1960s incarnation could not have been more different. Run by brothers Jeffrey and Harold Wallis, the store at Marble Arch had tremendous buying power and a reputation for innovation and risk taking, whilst still being firmly in the middle market. A visit to Woodstock Street from Harold Wallis and Pat Raphael, Wallis Shops' dress designer, gave Jean Varon its first large orders.

21

'Pat always advised Harold and she looked at a collection with a designer's eye. The look I showed that season was short and in fabrics not used in such a way at the time, lots of gingham and lace which I subsequently used a lot. She ordered forty-eight of a style which was unheard of – normally customers ordered one or two of a design.'

Jeffrey and Harold liked very avant-garde fashion for Marble Arch because it was by far the best shop in Oxford Street – nobody came close to Wallis Shops – which is hard to imagine these days. Wallis and Fenwick's used to compete to see who'd get the first copy from the French collections in their windows. Wallis were famous for their copies of the new season's Chanel suit which they bought from the French house each season. These copies were always a sell-out and caused queues to form outside the shop overnight. Jeffrey Wallis was responsible for coats and suits whilst Harold took care of dresses. They were wholesalers as well as retailers and had a very well-run factory on Boundary Road with efficient and well-trained staff. Monty Black, who later founded the luxury firm Baccarat and bought Wetherill, was their head cutter and worked closely with me later when I designed coats and suits for Wallis on an unattributed freelance basis.

17 Woodstock Street was a very small little house with four floors – we let the top off to a painter who was also a restorer for all the galleries in the area – it was wonderful – I was up and down there like a yo-yo. I was underneath, then it was the workroom, then the showroom. In the workroom were the machinists. Usually all the fabric that was coming in was kept in the room that I would design in – all undone as I liked to see what went with what – mine was the messy room!'

John employed machinists to make up the samples on site and the repeat orders for the shops. The size of the Wallis order meant they now had too many units to make in-house and yet still not enough to have made economically by an outworker. Each dress had to be cut individually and fitted on the stand by the machinist which was very time-consuming. 'We were always running late; wedding dresses for Fenwick's competing for space with dresses for Wallis and other customers – it was a nightmare, but better than having no orders at all. After a season of chaos we found some outworkers who were able to produce small quantities and employed a pattern cutter to grade, which made life a little easier. Out-workers usually wanted orders of at least 100 garments spread over not more than four sizes so this was a godsend to us.'

With Fenwick's and Wallis on board the continued success of John's designs long term still depended on the level of coverage in the press.

'The more press coverage we received the easier it was to write to potential clients. Sometimes successfully, often not, but I wasn't going to be beaten. The support of the fashion writers and magazines is so important in helping a fledgling designer. The enthusiastic encouragement given to me by Jane Humphries of *Flair* magazine and of Brigid Keenan, Mrs Carter's assistant on *The Sunday Times,* who lobbied like mad to get her to visit the showroom, forever puts me in their debt. Marit Allen and Caterine Milinaire of *Queen,* and Marit later at *Vogue* deserves a special mention for her gentle but determined way of making the extreme seem acceptable and normal. The only editor to write and thank me for showing her my collection! Marit almost single-handedly pushed the merits of London's young designers of that period to great success.'

Continued support from Ernestine Carter at *The Sunday Times* meant that other publications began to become more interested in the Jean Varon label, and features appeared in *Modern Woman, Flair, Vanity Fair* and increasingly day and evening wear in *Vogue.*

Over a relatively short period of time Wallis Shops had seen the reaction in the press and from their customers and approached John directly to work for them. 'I was offered a job at Wallis and I could have had "John Bates at Wallis Shops" as a brand, which was unheard of at the time. All the publicity to date had credited Jean Varon and I felt that I needed more recognition than the £8 a week I was receiving. I put my case to Eric West fairly forcibly and was given my name on all the publicity and a third share in the company.'

New materials, new shapes

2

In October 1962 *The Daily Sketch* featured the first hint of the innovation to come with the Jean Varon label: the PVC skirt. In two pieces, with a top in caramel wool the skirt was described as 'plastic patent'. Teamed with stiletto heeled boots from Anello and Davide the shape was still demure, with the hem just at the knee, but it marked a departure for the firm and the beginning of a period of intense innovation which was to establish the brand at the forefront of both mainstream design and clothes for younger fashion-conscious women. In a longer version for evening the pencil skirt in PVC teamed with a short evening bolero top merged both looks perfectly.

Still based in Woodstock Street, and later at Noel Street off Oxford Street, John had access to a wealth of small independent fabric and trim suppliers in Soho.

'There used to be shops which don't exist anymore – there was one that I passed and they had black PVC in the windows – it used to be used for café tablecloths. I would walk past on a daily basis and thought I must be able to incorporate that into something. I also used lace tablecloths – they were sold in squares so I had to think of a way of making it work for me. That's the way the design process starts off. The PVC didn't work because when we stitched it, it just came apart like a sheet of postage stamps. Luckily some fabric producers work with you and are open to suggestions – I'd ask "lets try and do this so it moulds to the body." As they kept on coming up with it, I kept using it. Nobody else would touch it.'

By the summer of 1963 Jean Varon was beginning to establish a regular clientele, and to gain full page features in the press, making the cover of *Woman's Mirror* in August with a dress modelled by Julie Christie, *Vanity Fair* in September and *Flair* in November.

Even at this relatively early stage of his design career a pattern emerges with John's collections which was to continue for the remainder of the company's history. On the one hand sleek, beautifully styled traditional day and evening dresses; ultimately very wearable and designed to appeal to a broad cross-section of clients, and on the other an undercurrent of change, gradually introducing new ideas and, when seen in the context of the history of 1960s fashion, pure innovation.

The shift dress and the empire line were two looks which John made his own during the early 1960s and were to become some of the best selling dresses of Jean Varon collections. Both styles relied on a classic, simple cut and could be accessorised with overstitched borders, a fabric flower or a bow, and both flattered a variety of figures.

A shift dress with bold black and brown horizontal stripes in wool featured in *The Sunday Times* in September 1963, cut just on the knee; its simplicity and geometry pre-date the mini dress but suggest a move towards a sharper, shorter shape. In contrast the elegant, longer empire line was one of the most popular and flattering designs for wedding dresses and eveningwear, two areas in which Jean Varon was establishing a reputation with traditional retailers and customers. One problem did persist with the public when selling the empire line for wedding dresses: 'A high waisted dress with a full skirt meant only one thing – look for the bride's father's shotgun.'

Opposite page
The classic shift dress, hinting at shorter shapes to come, as seen in *The Sunday Times*, September 1963.
Derek John/Fashion Museum, Bath

Left Bold innovation in materials: an evening skirt in black PVC for 1962, a material previously used only for rainwear and tablecloths.
Desmond Russell/John Bates

Right Summer 1963: Marguerites caught with yellow ribbon garland decorate the neck of a white slubbed rayon dress, selling at 14 guineas.
Fashion Museum, Bath

Vanity Fair featured a lace over satin empire line dress with huge fabric rose corsage on its cover that same month, and with a tiered, ruffled collar in *Modern Woman* in November the feel was Regency delicacy. Shown completely plain, in bright citrus crepe, the dresses became sleek and contemporary; or with hundreds of tiny fabric lilies-of-the-valley decorating the bodice as modelled by Jean Shrimpton in *The Sunday Times* in December, feminine and innocent. A version in pale pink organza with scattered appliqué flowers dusting the hem was to become a Jean Varon best-seller.

Opposite page
Jean Shrimpton models John's 'Lily of the Valley' dress, the bodice covered in hundreds of tiny flowerheads, 1964.
Norman Eales/Fashion Museum, Bath

May 1964: 'Fourposter', a tapering lace column dress with fluted sleeves and scallop edges, 21 guineas, together with a version of the 'Lily of the Valley' dress with sheer sleeves.
Norman Eales/Fashion Museum, Bath

John's innovative design for a culotte dress for Autumn/Winter 1963 was photographed with an erotic charge by Terence Donovan for *Queen* magazine, shown in yellow and black tweed with thigh high leather boots and described as 'almost a short dress'. Teaming shorts with a dress was to be adapted by John later in the decade, to solve the problem of ever-receding hemlines and modesty, with the look lengthened for the first bridal 'catsuit' in lace and silk jersey in early 1964. In white linen, culottes were worn with a simple tabard in citrus orange, or in white lace, described by the *Observer* as 'hostess pyjamas.'

A bold new idea for 1964 saw dresses teamed with stockings, using the same fabric for the legs, or taking elements of the trim and scattering the legs with appliqué. Brigid Keenan was the first to feature images in *The Sunday Times* in May: a dense floral print on a rayon jersey shift dress or in plain white embroidered with pendant beads – stockings and the dress retailing together at Wallis Shops and selected department stores at twenty-five guineas.

The style was immediately taken up by the press; it was easily photographed to great effect and truly original. With a matching headscarf total coordination arrived. Sarah Miles modelled one of the most beautiful versions in *Vogue* in August featuring a simple white dress and stockings decorated with pale pink silk roses. In the autumn collections John had adapted the look to include polka dots and zebra stripes.

Opposite page
Sarah Miles wears a Jean Varon rose decorated dress and matching stockings for *Vogue,* shot by David Bailey, September 1964.
David Bailey/Vogue. © The Condé Nast Publications Ltd

Above 'A dramatic dress in printed rayon jersey, patterned from head to foot and caught at the wrists and round the hood by black fox. What? Stockings too?' *Vogue* heralds the arrival of John's new prints retailing at 21 guineas.
Traeger/Vogue. © The Condé Nast Publications Ltd

Right Barney Wan's illustration for *Vogue* in June 1964 combined a romantic Jean Varon dress and a 'Midsummer's Night' setting.
Barney Wan

Far right 'Almost a short dress' in yellow and black tweed, shot by Terence Donovan for Queen.
Terence Donovan/National Magazines

A Jean Varon first: Grace Coddington
models dresses with stockings to
match, in tiny floral print or with
pendant appliqués.
Norman Eales/Fashion Museum, Bath

By now an awareness of the body beneath the clothes was becoming apparent in fashion shoots and editorials, a development which was ultimately to steer fashion towards a shorter hemline by the end of the year. First on the new body-aware scene was John with cut-out knees on trousers, featured in the *Daily Mirror* in September as 'keyhole kneeholes' and 'Great for a party, best in white and blue' according to model Pattie Boyd, sold in what the paper described as 'switched-on shops' at fifteen guineas.

Jean Varon's lower neckline was described as a 'perilously tiny bodice' by *Nova* magazine in the same month. Getting the dress photographed by the mainstream press as designed was a persistent problem for John, and it was not unusual for dresses with low necklines to be photographed pulled up from the back for a more modest décolletage.

One of the most important dresses from this period was called 'Ad Lib' after the popular London nightclub of the time. Combining two John Bates hallmarks in one dress the bodice was in a vest-like mesh with a grosgrain skirt and tiny bra, and as journalist Brigid Keenan described at the time it was 'only for the most daring dollies to wear in the hottest discotheques.'

'No woman should wear a foundation, they're ugly and uncomfortable', John was quoted as saying in the *Daily Sketch* in December 1964 and it is this ethic which became increasingly important in the way that Jean Varon clothes were designed. Ironically it would be the 'bra dress' which ensured that John's designs stayed in the limelight, provoking widespread coverage and debate on the suggestion of underwear as outerwear.

The Sun asked 'Why go to the party in your pyjamas when you look even more delectable in your undies?' and used the nineteen year-old Jane Birkin as a model. The design, a simple lace over satin bra teamed with a matching skirt with bow at the waist, featured in countless articles but provoked the kind of publicity any designer would relish. By the close of 1964 *Honey* magazine put it simply: 'How far will you go?'

Top 'Ad Lib', named after a London nightclub, with panels of crepe and sheer mesh; revealing and concealing.
David Montgomery/National Magazines

'How far will you go?' The bra dress on the cover of *Honey* for January 1965: underwear as outerwear arrives.
Anthony Norris/IPC Magazines

The Little Girl Shape for Spring' was how the *Daily Express* announced the arrival of the defining look of a decade in November 1964. John's sketch of a simple shift dress, cut-away at the armholes and with angled pockets was not announced as anything other than a new take on the youthful, body-conscious dresses being previewed for the following spring, but many would argue that this was the birth of the mini dress in the mainstream press.

The movement of hemlines upwards and the ensuing scramble to claim authorship of the look has caused continual debate for over forty years, but what is clear from this design is that it is truly unlike anything that had gone before, whether from other British designers or the Paris catwalks. It inverts the established ideal of womanly sophistication; to be fashionable from this point on is to be young, daring, risqué.

An element of the success of John's designs could be put down to his ability to predict and accentuate a mood in fashion. With the mini dress he went beyond simply raising hemlines of an existing look as many of his contemporaries did; instead he designed the shortest, sharpest mini dresses of the decade.

When you're designing there's always something in the air, and designers pick up on this in their own particular way. Mine were the shortest dresses, put it that way.'

When Ernestine Carter reviewed fashion in the '60s for *The Sunday Times* in December 1969, she chose a Courreges dress from 1964 at three inches above the knee and another from 1969 at eight inches above to illustrate the article. Next to it she put a Patrick Hunt shot of a Jean Varon mini dress from 1967 at ten inches above the knee. A long time supporter of John, there was no contest in her mind as to which dress defined the look of the decade.

Little girl shape for spring

THE SHAPE OF '65. John Bates, young British designer who is extremely shape-conscious, sketches his Little Girl Shape for spring. The back shows, the underarms show—and lots of leg shows.

A defining moment —1965 and The Avengers

'Mrs Peel – we're needed!' Diana Rigg previews designs for the show with John Bates.
Fashion Museum, Bath

To say that that 1965 was an important year for Jean Varon would be an understatement for it marked the beginning of an unprecedented level of growth for the company and a media frenzy surrounding John's designs for Diana Rigg in *The Avengers*.

Honor Blackman had just left the show for James Bond and, as her leather-clad look by Frederick Starke had been so successful, designers on the show were assuming that Diana Rigg's Emma Peel would continue in the same vein. Before filming of the new series was even half way through ABC realised this was a mistake, as the look missed the new vitality of the character. Out of the blue John was approached by Anne Trehearne, an ex-editor of *Queen* magazine, to produce designs for the show. 'They'd offered it to Jean Muir first and, fortunately for me, she had been unable or unwilling to meet the TV company's deadline – and if you don't deliver on a film or television set then it's panic time for them.'

In the event John had four days to produce designs before the first episode, on an actress he'd never met before. 'When you're starting off designing for a new girl you've got to know the figure, really quite intimately, so you can see how you can present that figure at its very best and not detract from it. Maybe it was a good idea to be in such a rush – it concentrated the mind.'

The designs proved to be some of the most memorable of the decade, cut to be fresh, young and eminently suitable for an action heroine. In an era of black and white television, they also translated beautifully to the small screen, themed around a basic two-tone palette and incorporating many of the looks which Jean Varon were already producing commercially. The collection included coordinated skirt and trouser suits, 'fighting suits', op-art fur coats, bold shift dresses with contrast stripes, vinyl double breasted 'car coats', a white crepe plunge neck dress with Cossack embroidery and elegant empire line evening dresses with guipure-lace bodices, gathered high under the bust.

As with all Jean Varon designs each was named, sometimes with a hint of irony. 'It's impudent, erotic – I like it,' said Patrick MacNee of 'Flash', a gleaming turquoise lamé outfit of hipsters, bra and short jacket retailing at twenty-nine guineas.

'Belt-up' and 'Black Bottom' were fighting suits in Celon stretch jersey at seventen guineas a piece and 'HQ' was a long sleeved dress in white crepe with red and navy embroidery. 'Hill' was a black and white wool coat designed to be worn and coordinated with 'Calvary', a shift dress with bold braid cross design. Even lingerie was included with a negligee called 'Mystery and Imagination' at three pounds, ten shillings and sixpence.

Sleek, confident and not without
humour: Diana Rigg models some of
the most iconic clothes of the decade
for *The Sunday Times* in 1965.
David Gittings/ The Sunday Times

Diana Rigg
"The Avengers"

Silver grey/blue
soft lamé.
jkt, bra, +
hipsters.

JOHN BATES.

DIANA RIGG
"THE AVENGERS"

BLACK LEATHER
CATSUIT BUCKLED
TO ONE SIDE.
CREPE ROLL NECK
SHIRT IN WHITE.

JOHN BATES.

DIANA RIGG.
"THE AVENGERS"

EVENING DRESS
WITH GUIPURE
LACE TOP +
STOLE.
The GUIPURE
lace shoes.

JOHN BATES.

Diana Rigg
"The Avengers"

Short B/W ②
coney coat.

to go
over
fighting suits
(black stretch
jersey).

Diana Rigg
"The Avengers"

Grey "lizard"
coat   short.
To be worn
with or without
trousers.

JOHN BATES.

Diana Rigg.

The Avengers

JOHN BATES.

Diana Rigg
"The Avengers"

Black + White
crepe "catsuit"

JOHN BATES.

Diana Rigg

"THE AVENGERS"

SHORT B/W
CONEY COAT.

JOHN BATES.

Diana Rigg
"The Avengers"

Black + White
coat with
reversed
decoration of
faille ribbon.

JOHN BATES.

In a further ground-breaking move Jean Varon licensed a number of firms to produce individual elements of the collection for sale nationwide through boutiques and department stores. Coats and suits were made by Reginald Bernstein, the jersey fighting suits and the crepe and lace catsuits by Simon Ellis, leather and rainwear by Paul Blanche, fur coats by Selincourt, lingerie by Charnos, Echo for stockings (John had wanted patterned tights so that Emma Peel could fight in her dress if necessary, but manufacturers had declined the product suggesting the concept was impractical), gloves were by Dents, handbags by Freedex, target motif berets by Kangol, and even an Avengers watch by Jean Varon, with a target dial, from Freedman.

Getting what John had designed to be worn on screen as he intended was another matter. 'I delivered one particular design and they came back to me asking "Where's Miss Rigg's costume?" The stunt man had worn it and ripped it to shreds. We had to start all over again.'

ABC also took a traditional view on the issue of rising hemlines, with John's designs often considered far too short for television. 'I quickly realised that the hems were being let down because they were considered to be too short on set. So, instead of turning up the hem in the usual way, I cut the exact length and stitched a false hem so they couldn't be "let down". Annie Trehearne and I visited the set very early on in the shooting and we stopped off in an empty hangar at the studios for me to pin up her skirt 10 inches above the knee. I think the taxi driver thought he was in the middle of a *Carry On* film. She then walked onto the set with great aplomb as if it were the most natural thing in the world to wear skirts that short, and to universal approbation of the technicians. We didn't have any more problems!'

The press went wild, with blanket coverage of the Avengers collection in every major British newspaper and magazine. *Vogue* featured the selected designs modelled by Jean Shrimpton in October 1965 and in all over 150 articles featuring the collection were to make appearances in British and foreign journals.

'All the nationals covered the clothes – talk about "I've arrived" – you just opened up the papers and there were whole great columns – by all the fashion editors – they'd been looking forward wondering what was going to be done, but they hadn't seen anything. When it came to it they all pulled out the stops – it was amazing. It made my name at the time, but I wouldn't do another series – I had too many things to do.'

What is clear from reading contemporary reporting is the way in which the clothes perfectly matched Diana Rigg's character, and how much young women were looking for a role model. Sleek, confident and not without humour could be used to describe Emma Peel and so too John's designs. On 27 September 1965 Felicity Green in the *Daily Mirror* wrote 'The question, the morning after, will undoubtedly be: Did you see what Emma wore – and where can I buy it?'

Promoted with special trade fashion shows in London in August 1965, the success of the collection led to an unforeseen problem for Jean Varon and ABC television. In early 1966 the newspapers began reporting on the beginnings of a shop war, as hundreds of copies of Avengers clothing started to appear. ABC, which got a percentage of sales, began sending warning letters to shops selling clothes purporting to be genuine Avengers designs.

Press coverage of the designs continued well into 1966 as the episodes unfolded on television. With the success of the show came a heightened media interest in the designer which was to remain in place for the next fifteen years and guaranteed that the Jean Varon brand was now firmly at the forefront of British fashion.

Opposite page
John Bates's sketches for Diana Rigg as Emma Peel, using a simple two tone palette and crisp, modern lines.
John Bates

The cover of a 1965 brochure promoting the Avengers collection, featuring the Terry O'Neill shoot of Rigg and Patrick MacNee.
Terry O'Neill/John Bates

If the Avengers collection dominated the thoughts of a new generation of television watchers in late 1965, it was 'op-art' and the controversy of rising hemlines that filled countless articles in the fashion magazines for the remainder of the year. For John the success of the collection brought vast amounts of new publicity, but the core of the business was not neglected and he continued to produce radical new designs.

January 1965 saw John's terracotta and navy dress with mesh midriff photographed by Duffy for *Vogue*. Modelled by Jean Shrimpton, the dress was to be chosen by the Fashion Writers' Association as dress of the year for the Museum of Costume in Bath, with shoes by Anello and Davide – it was an inspired choice as the design perfectly represents several moods concurrent in fashion at the time. The mini was yet to be adopted universally yet the design points to an increased sexual charge in dressing, with the bared midriff and low cut neckline. At the same time it is perfectly demure, nothing is overtly over-emphasised – a skill which was the key to Jean Varon's success in producing clothes whose designs increasingly ran in parallel to each other, maximising the client base and financial success.

Felicity Green writing for the *Daily Mirror* in Spring 1965 gave Jean Varon the sort of publicity any fashion house would kill for with her snappily titled 'The Smallest Dress in the World' featuring John's design for a 'half bra' top decorated with flowers and matching skirt, both in denim. What is important in the context of the period is that the paper sought to draw its readers' attention to the risqué elements of the design, but was generally supportive of the innovation. It was editors like Felicity Green of the *Daily Mirror,* Ernestine Carter of *The Sunday Times* and Barbara Griggs at the *Evening Standard* that kept Jean Varon dresses in the headlines.

Increasingly, the clothes were shot by some of the world's leading photographers including Terence Donovan, Terry O'Neill, David Bailey and Cecil Beaton, who understood how John envisaged the clothes being worn and accessorised. Regular appearances in *Vogue* became the norm, with Jean Varon designs being featured at every level, whether it be bridal, in 'Young Ideas' or for opulent empire line evening wear.

The smallest dress in the world

Opposite page
'Kasbah', modelled by Jean Shrimpton for *Vogue* in January 1965 and chosen as 'Dress of the Year' at the Museum of Costume in Bath by the Fashion Writers' Association.
Duffy/Vogue. © The Condé Nast Publications Ltd

John Bates at work in 1965, with 'Chosen by Vogue' cards increasingly covering the studio.
John Bates

Cutout panels were a natural progression from bare midriffs and the sheer panels of 'Kasbah' and 'Ad Lib', shot by Duffy for *Queen* magazine in pink and white gingham seersucker. *Duffy/National Magazines*

Below left At the ancient palace of Knossos, a baby-doll dress of striped cotton organdie worn over black Bermudas in rayon jersey. *David Gittings/National Magazines*

Below right Jean Varon designs had begun to make waves across the channel by 1965, as featured here in the April edition of *Jardin des Modes*.

The daisy dress was to become a Jean Varon classic, with bold appliqué daisies, bigger, bolder and more daring than any other to date, and a natural progression from the lily-of-the-valley decorated dresses of the previous year. Shirley Anne Field modelled the empire line version on the cover of *Nova* magazine in May and Jean Varon gained more column inches in the press when ten debutantes arrived at a May Ball in Cambridge wearing versions of the same dress. Taking the co-ordinated look a step further, an alternative ensemble included sleek cropped bolero top, slim full length skirt and daisy-covered bonnet.

Ernestine Carter noted a 1920s feel to some of the day dresses showing for spring in *The Sunday Times* in late 1964 and the theme developed throughout the year with pencil pleated, tiered shifts in bright yellow rayon or pale pink crepe showing from Jean Varon. With dramatic horizontal stripes the feel was contemporary, but with a bow at the hip or bust the dress became understated and chic.

Combining column skirt, cropped sleeveless bodice and matching head gear, the total look for 1965, modelled in the Jean Varon studio.
Don Price/John Bates

Fashion goes trans-Atlantic aboard the QE2

In October 1965, as part of the 14th London Fashion week, an estimated 700 fashion buyers from forty countries around the globe came to the capital to see the best of British fashion, organised by the London Fashion House Group and shown at the Hilton Hotel ballroom on Park Lane. Jean Varon showed op-art dresses four inches above the knee, incorporating features such as ribbed stockings, which were so popular with *The Avengers* and which guaranteed more headlines in the fashion press. A simple empire line evening dress in black and white spots with a daringly low cut neckline was described by the *Belfast Telegraph* as 'breath-taking' and was to feature prominently in an American promotion also organised by the group a few days later.

As part of a government-sponsored export drive seventeen British ready-to-wear manufacturers set sail on the QE2 for New York, each taking with them a capsule collection to show to American buyers. Cunard built a catwalk and provided the lighting, Ralph Stroh and Paul Mitchell at Vidal Sassoon did the hair and Yardley the make-up. The exhibitors included Jean Varon, Digby Morton, Frederick Starke (who had provided the costumes for Honor Blackman in *The Avengers*), Cojana, Jean Allen, Frank Usher, Simon Massey, Burberry and Wallis for a show entitled 'British Fashions – USA '66'.

The American press loved every moment with the *New York Times* declaring, on 5th November, 'The British Have Arrived'. The Jean Varon show was entirely in black and white showing the shortest skirts of the exhibitors. Caroline Combe for the *Daily Mail* reported that the notoriously conservative American buyers were left goggling. Nancy White, editor in chief of *Harper's Bazaar* was quoted as saying 'A fabulous show, the best I've ever seen' and one buyer asked 'Are all these short dresses for the children's department?' The star of the show was a Jean Varon catsuit trimmed with ostrich feathers, which the *Mail* reported had Eugenia Shepherd of the *New York Herald Tribune* 'feverishly writing notes'.

Several models went ashore wearing miniskirts, reported the *New York Times*. 'It was ghastly, we were whistled at and mobbed.' Sales, however, were strong, as buyers later journeyed to the Plaza Hotel to place orders, before the show transferred to the Pacific coast.

Eric West and John Bates at Woodstock Street, 1965.
John Bates/Keystone Press Agency

Down by the quay, Jean Shrimpton wears an op-art ensemble which was to take America by storm aboard the QE2. John Bates stands over her shoulder.
Vernier/Telegraph Media Group

65 for 66
for
jean
VARON

piebald horse
effect. OK.
Insert black
on to white
linen.

Opposite page
Op-art bursts into *Vogue*, shot at
Shepherd Market in Mayfair with
amazed glances from the crowd, the
dresses available from November
1965 at 12 guineas.
*Traeger/Vogue © The Condé Nast
Publications Ltd*

John's bold designs for 1965 in a two
tone palette were unlike anything seen
before, and allowed him to develop a
look begun on screen in *The Avengers*,
with co-ordinated dress, stockings
and shoes.
John Bates

The great hem debate – a new geometry in fashion

'Can skirts get any shorter?' asked Barbara Griggs in the *Evening Standard* in the autumn of 1965. 'Yes' was the answer from Jean Varon. Again ahead of the field John showed a loose fitting bold organza mini dress with geometric grid design in gold, and five inches above the knee, over a tiny 'culotte' dress in black Tricel jersey retailing at fourteen guineas. It made it to 'Young Ideas' in *Vogue* and a full page in *Flair*. By the end of the year the mini was a firm favourite for the look of 1966.

The Avengers collection and these new, daring dresses had picked up on a mood in fashion that was to dominate the next few years and indeed eventually invert the traditional model of couture as the sole inspiration of what sold in the British High Street and in the new generation of boutiques for younger clients.

By providing an alternative to stockings and traditional foundation garments with his culotte underdresses, Jean Varon met head-on the problems of the shorter look. In spring 1966, to take total coordination a step further, the firm previewed a new range of nightwear for Charnos.

The collection included 'Trixie', a bra and long skirt set in cotton at two pounds, two shillings. Quoted in *The Sunday Times* in December 1965 John stated 'My night dresses are absolutely non-fussy, but aimed to make the girl inside look pretty.'

Some were quite conventional, some brought new ideas such as bra tops, elasticated at the back, teamed with hipster shorts that tied under the navel, and long sarong wrap skirts with a tie at one side.

Even this was relevant to mainstream design for it complemented the 'Baby Doll' look – a new shape for day and evening wear in the form of a trapeze-cut, shorter mini dress with high waistlines which hit the press by mid-1966.

Jean Varon showed delicate lace mini dresses with scallop hems, and a tiered version with sequin borders was shot for the *Evening News* in May. 'Sweet' was how Barbara the model described it in the shoot 'but they'll never wear it at this length in the States' (five inches above the knee). Skirts in New York were still at mid-knee level.

The shirt dress, a bold, simple shape, one of the most iconic looks of the '60s, featured in 'Young Ideas' in *Vogue* in April '66; a development of the shift dress into a versatile day or evening dress with buttons at the collars and cuffs and perhaps a belt at hip level. John's designs came in flannel, wool or cotton, in a

Above Short and sweet, the vitality of the new length caught for French magazine *Jardin des Modes*.
Jardin des Modes

Jean Varon designs feature in a promotion for Celon, one of a new generation of synthetic fibres increasingly popular by the mid-1960s.

Left Hipster shorts and bra top in white lawn printed with flowers, and a similar version with long sarong tied skirt: two nightwear designs by John for Charnos, drawn by Christian Bernais.
Fashion Museum, Bath

cavalcade of colours, with or without decorative top stitching, contrast collars or, available by July that year, in textured silver as 'Sterling', which merged the shirt dress and futuristic metallics.

Woman's Mirror picked up the enduring versatility of the dress and featured three versions in a photo shoot with models of differing ages – from short in navy blue with lipstick red tights and shoes, to a longer length on the knee for a more mature buyer. 'I'm always hearing complaints that current fashion is directed at just one type, but that's nonsense', he said. 'I have three different types of girl in the photograph to model the same design, but in different colours and skirt lengths.'

Regardless of the extensive and very positive coverage of Jean Varon's shorter styles in the press and fashion magazines, selling dresses at the 'sample' length (i.e. the length which the designer envisaged) was often far from easy, as John had already encountered when dressing Diana Rigg on *The Avengers* set. In May '66 Felicity Green reported on the battle of the hemlines in an article for the *Daily Mirror*, using a Jean Varon metallic silver shirt dress with wide hipster belt as illustration of the variations in orders across the globe. Orders for the shortest version came from Sweden and a single boutique in London and New York. Then came London and the provinces along with the majority of Europe, and, at what was described as 'miserable No. 3', the west coast stores of America.

In July of the same year *The Sunday Times Magazine* cover story by Meriel McCooey featured a pair of shapely legs marked with a league table of skirt lengths from designers. Out in front with the shortest skirts was John Bates, followed by Mary Quant and Gerald McCann in second and third. Interestingly, in last place – Yves St Laurent.

If some buyers were reluctant to order skirts as John had designed them this never affected the order book, as his designs could be adapted to match the stores' or boutiques' wishes. The client was always right which meant that whilst Jean Varon dresses remained in the headlines, on a practical level the company was able to sell to a wide audience through a network of department stores and independent boutiques. The range of dresses featured in the press illustrate perfectly the way in which the designs catered for more than one group of buyers, offering the adaptable shift and empire line dress alongside vibrant 'Baby Dolls' and the briefest of minis. What emerged by the second half of 1966 was that Jean Varon designs were out in front when it came to the great hem debate, but innovation was far from over.

Winning designs from the 1966 'London Look' award in the USA: 'Sterling' in brilliant reflecting silver and 'Wednesday' with three tiers edged in sequins, selling at $90 and $85.
Jay Maisel

Fashion in motion: a tiny PVC mini dress with clear Perspex hem inset, shot for *Vogue* by Helmut Newton; visor and head gear by James Wedge.
Helmut Newton/Vogue © The Condé Nast Publications Ltd

Ever since his PVC evening skirt in 1962 John had been experimenting with avant-garde materials he had managed to source in the wholesale trade suppliers in and around Berwick Street in London's Soho. 1966 saw the results of some of this research in a riot of neon and brightly coloured PVC; in raincoats, in mini dresses and in accessories. *Vogue's* coverage in April saw models in motion in PVC – on a racing bike with tiny dress with orange perspex hem, teamed with a close-fitting helmet and visor by James Wedge. July brought a bevy of models dressed in fluorescent Jean Varon PVC mini dresses in a double-page shoot aboard a boat.

Interestingly, even ground-breaking coverage such as this still implied a practical reason for using PVC and it would be some time before its association with rainwear diminished. Coverage in the press mirrored the designs themselves with the mini dresses photographed on waif-like models like Twiggy and Penelope Tree, the longer evening dresses purveying womanly, sophisticated elegance.

'Venice' was a perfect example of the latter and one of the company's most popular and versatile designs of the Sixties. A simple empire line dress in crepe with ribbon appliqué over the bust and around the hem, it was available in a range of plain colours, or in electric combinations such as lime and pale blue, retailing at sixteen and a half guineas. The dress was pretty enough to wear to a party, and formal enough to be a wedding dress in ivory and white; the press called it 'high empire line' referring to the smaller, more revealing bust line, first seen in the QE2 show a year before.

> 'Venice had a very low neckline but was perfectly safe because of the fit and a girl didn't need to wear a bra with it. Indeed couldn't. At one stage it was impossible to sell a dress that wasn't lined; buyers would ask "what are my customers going to wear underneath?"'

An explosion of vinyl colour – neon, electric and metallic

Opposite page
'Venice' in ribbon decorated crepe proved to be one of the most popular Jean Varon designs of the 1960s, available in plain colours and a variety of contrasting combinations
John Bates

Sheer innovation: John with Twiggy, modelling his transparent mini dress with silver hem and matching shorts.
Barry Lategan

John's innovations were rewarded in July when he won the Yardley 'London Look' award, given each year to the young British designer deemed to have shown the most creativity and presented at the Plaza Hotel in New York. In the fashion show accompanying the ceremony Jean Varon showed a riot of 'barer than bare' PVC mini dresses. The *Oldham Evening Chronicle* later reported enthusiastically that the models wore 'beige moisture tint foundation for the natural look, white oyster eye shadow above the lid, silver grey close to the lashes, pink lips paled and glossed with a frosty polished lipstick.'

Promotion followed promotion. In the US John appeared in San Francisco as part of the 'Britain Today' campaign and nine of the city's stores opened 'Carnaby Street' boutiques for men and women. With six model girls in tow he took the look of swinging London to the Riviera in August, showing at the Palm Beach Casino in Nice. It was an instant success, with guests including King Hussein of Jordan paying thirty-five guineas a ticket. 'We're knocking them rigid down here,' said Anne Lambton, fashion consultant, with a second show televised the following night from Mr Paul Pucci's nightclub. The French press revelled at the PVC 'minirobes' and bystanders stared at the models' pale faces and risqué hemlines as they rode through the town on a fire engine.

Autumn was dominated by the short, sharp tunic dress, in neon crepe photographed by Terence Donovan for *Flair,* in shimmering silver modelled by Twiggy in *Vogue's* 'Young Ideas' in September, or as a scarlet PVC slip with cutaway arms and buttons on the shoulders in November. Norman Parkinson captured the versatility of the shape in John's daring mini wedding dress and chiffon veil for *Vogue,* available at Fenwick's at nineteen guineas.

Felicity Green predicted trends for 1967 in the *Daily Mirror* in December: 'It's the French wholesale firms – along with Britain's Quant, Muir, Bates, Tuffin and Foale et al – who now provide us with all the exciting ideas that the Paris high fashion houses, with a couple of noteworthy exceptions, try hard to copy.'

wedding
eil,
kinson
eas.

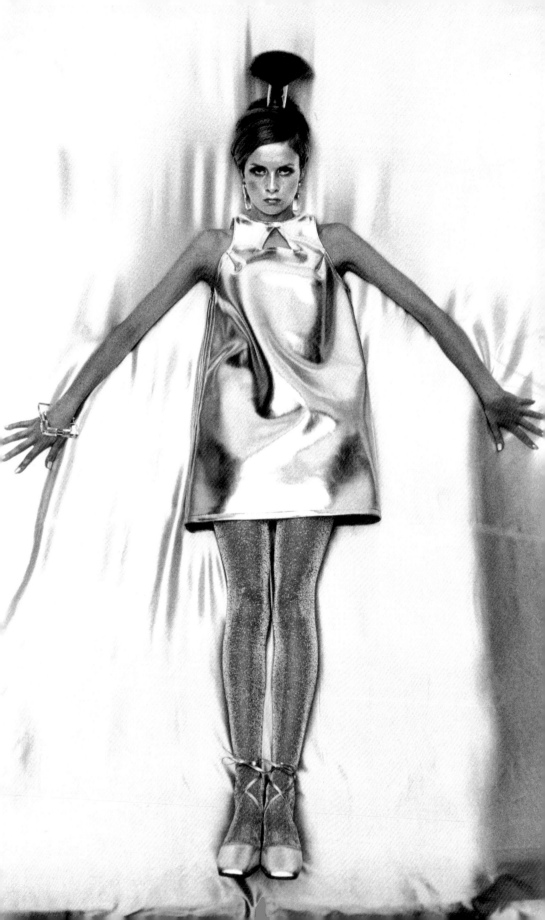

Retail
revolution

By the end of 1966, as a result of employing a professional sales manager to run the showroom in Woodstock Street and the resulting surge in sales, it was felt necessary to move to larger premises. The company took a long term lease on 19-20 Noel Street; over 6,500 square feet of offices, workrooms and showrooms, and in the heart of the West End.

John was steadily building a team of trusted professionals around him vital to a designer. Susan Jarrett the sales manager in question was a woman of considerable skill and experience, having worked for Polly Peck, a well-established wholesale house, for a number of years. Her client book was impressive and customers who were previously 'unavailable' began to visit the showroom and order. She was also an invaluable and dispassionate link between the customer and designer. Judith Allera, who had joined the company as a model/assistant in Woodstock Street, was now responsible for production as well as still fitting the first samples and modelling. Stephanie Tartakoff, who John renamed 'Titch', was employed as another showroom model and sales assistant and was a hit with customers. Doris Lewsey was a brilliant pattern cutter who could cut straight into fabric from John's sketches with amazing accuracy. To liaise with the press and promote the brand John Siggins was engaged as a freelance PR. It was an inspired team which was to remain in place for years to come.

The biggest, and hardest, retailers to crack still remained the department stores. To gain a foothold with them meant nationwide distribution but even if their buyers did pay a visit to the new Jean Varon showrooms they were constrained in what they could buy by rigid budgets. 'Quite often they would say "I would love to buy but I've spent my budget for the season"'. 'Sale or Return' was one way round this problem and whilst the company was reluctant to get too deeply involved, it was a way of selling stock that had to be made to make the production of a particular style economical. This in turn led to the forerunner of the 'Shop in Shop' for Jean Varon, which at this stage amounted to no more than a showcase or rail within a department. 'In the late 1960s we had a handful of such units, run by a redoubtable lady of the old school named Mrs Josef, always immaculately turned out; hair scraped back in a chignon, wonderful make-up and jewellery. I renamed her "Fred"'.

Opposite page/following spread
For Autumn/Winter 1967 Twiggy models the Jean Varon short, full cape, worn with shorts as an alternative to a mini.
Just Jaekin/Vogue © The Condé Nast Publications Ltd

Fashions diverge

The second half of the 1960s brought a gradual yet nonetheless important change in mood characterised by a divergence of styles. Spring 1967 brought softer smocking and prints to mini dresses, and the cape as an alternative to coats. Twiggy modelled 'neat pleats' in *Vogue* in February and by May a nostalgic seersucker smock in a tiny cottage garden floral. John used a dramatic slashed sleeve detail, and a dropped waist figured in Ernestine Carter's editorial in *The Sunday Times*, predicting 'New Capes, New Shirt-waisters, New Lace and New Sleeves'. Needless to say all the dresses illustrated were Jean Varon designs.

The minis were ultra-short and bold, or in soft chiffons with gathered cuffs and lace or flower appliqué trim. Cecil Beaton photographed Twiggy for *Vogue* in an iconic yellow velvet mini shift with roll collar which combined impish charm and a cutting edge modernity; from the same shoot, a drop-waisted dark green velvet slip of a dress was the shortest taboo-breaking Varon to date.

Asked by *Drapery and Fashion Weekly* how he saw his collections for '67/'68 John was characteristically specific: '…lots of pleats, dresses cut on a square inspired by the Chinese ballet, masses of jersey, demure high necked granny dresses with ruffles, tent shapes, belted either high or low, the nude look, using crochet in new ways, jewel embroidery in crushed stone colourings, brown, black and chocolate colours.'

Risk-taking was always an element of John's collections, now held in his smart new West End showroom. It was no coincidence that the designs which grabbed the headlines as daring or risqué were a guarantee of publicity for the remainder of the collections which were designed with a wider audience in mind. John Siggins recalls 'I used to ask John to give me three Cosmopolitan dresses a season regardless of what else he was designing, on the principle that sex sells and quite often clients would come in as a result of the publicity they generated and finish up buying something very different from the collection.'

Opposite page
The new lace: a square of Calais lace over white taffeta, shoulder bows in black satin. £13 2s 6d
Patrick Hunt/Fashion Museum, Bath.

The new cape: circular, tab fronted, high collared in red wool crepe with matching shorts. 18 guineas.
Patrick Hunt/Fashion Museum, Bath.

Opposite page

The new shirtwaister: window pane checks in pink, blue, green and yellow, the turned up collar line in yellow to match the low drawstring belt. £6 19s 6d. *Patrick Hunt/Fashion Museum, Bath.*

The new sleeve: slashed to the long cuffs in purple bouclé wool, on a dress with wide buckled belt. £10 9s 6d. *Patrick Hunt/Fashion Museum, Bath.*

The trouser suit debate rumbled on and a striking design for evening first appeared in December, with editorials spilling over into spring 1968. In rich purple moire velvet, the hipster trousers and matching waistcoat were shown with a lace trimmed blouse; a dandy look which ran parallel to a 'Puritan' collar on evening dresses. Still banned in the dining rooms of hotels such as the Savoy and Claridge's, the trouser suit grabbed the headlines again by the summer as debutante and showjumper Jayne Harris was refused entry to the Royal Enclosure at Ascot, wearing a trouser suit by the boutique Quorum. She promptly changed into a tiny lace mini dress from Jean Varon, as short as the jacket on the suit, and was granted entry. The press approved.

Opposite page
Photographed by Cecil Beaton for *Vogue*, Twiggy models a Jean Varon mini dress in yellow velvet, with hems continuing their journey skywards into 1967.
Sotheby's/Cecil Beaton Archive

Above Black linen shift, laced up the front with orange braid. £8 4s.
Fashion Museum, Bath

Right An alternative to the shorter look: a romantic lace and organza evening dress for 1967, the neck and high waist tied with lilac satin ribbon. 22 guineas.
Norman Eales/Fashion Museum, Bath.

'A dress is a prop, no more – it's the way that she wears it that counts' said John, interviewed by *Model Girl* in February. Cilla Black agreed and promoted her new Jean Varon wardrobe later that month, designed for her television show. In theatrical and glamorous designs, she modelled a white jersey trouser suit with high collar encrusted with rhinestones, with a swag of crystal beads at the waist. The collection was not available in shops like the Avengers but shared the need to be as versatile. Diana Rigg had to fight and stash a pistol, Cilla had to look good on camera from all angles, change easily between numbers and dance.

John had met Cilla through Eric West who knew Peter Brown, the Beatles manager Brian Epstein's personal assistant, who was later to become a partner in the tailor Tommy Nutter's business. She chose a specially made Jean Varon mini dress for her church wedding to Bobby Willis that year, the cuffs trimmed with floating ostrich feathers, and the regular interviews she carried out centring on her glamorous wardrobe ensured that the Jean Varon name shared the limelight.

Opposite page
June 1967: from 'Young Ideas' in *Vogue*, 'smallest yellow crepe tunic with greatest electric effect', skinny scooped top, side buttons, and a tiny skirt with drawstring tie. 11 guineas.
David Bailey/Vogue © The Condé Nast Publications Ltd

Designs for a star: John had been introduced to Cilla Black through a contact in Brian Epstein's office and his fresh, modern designs for her TV shows provided superb publicity for Jean Varon.
John Bates

A trio of dresses for spring introduced new sheer panels to eveningwear. 'Bunny' in black and white crepe had sheer side panels with embroidered braid, 'Polo', for obvious reasons, a central circle and 'Eve' replaced the mesh panels of 'Ad Lib' with sheer chiffon for the barest of looks. The shortest of dresses came in chiffon tiers, or decorated with rainbow dyed tassels. Culottes and pant suits complemented the longer, more nostalgic look which was beginning to win the battle of the hemlines and by the end of the year John was designing floor length jersey culotte dresses teamed with PVC waistcoats, and Matador jackets in bolero lengths with military collars decorated with braid.

'The look is as bare as possible without being vulgar – mostly for evening. Fabrics will be transparent, and there'll be masses of feathers: little broody hen speckled feathers on dresses and accessories too – and there'll be plenty of trousers' was John's view of 1969 quoted in the *Daily Express* in December. True to form, the first headline-grabbing dress of the year was 'Hitchcock' featuring a sheer top and two 'hands' of feathers covering the bust, retailing at eighteen pounds, six shillings.

Opposite page
A step on from 'Ad Lib': a mini dress with alternating bands of crepe and sheer georgette.
John Adriaan/Daily Mirror

Above The 'little girl look': linen mini dress with wide hipster belt, circa 1968.
John Bates

Right Tiers of toning tassels: Jean Shrimpton spends some time with herself in a Jean Varon mini dress, shot for *Vogue*.
David Bailey/Vogue © The Condé Nast Publications Ltd

Collaboration, coats, suits and the new luxury

The final year of the decade was again marked by a variety of styles running in parallel. The mini dresses were as short as ever, but the impact of the trouser suit, the maxi length and a new, Victorian, buttoned-up sophistication in eveningwear and coats was beginning to make its mark. 'Rating' took a plunging neckline to new extremes, available with culotte style trousers or a full circle skirt. The halterneck top was kept in place by horizontal ties under the bust, fastening almost like a bra to the back.

The previous year John had collaborated with both Boutique Furs, designing a range of coats, and the new luxury wholesale firm Baccarat, owned by Monty Black, whom he knew from his work with Wallis Shops almost a decade earlier. Along with a select group of other designers he produced beautifully constructed coats in suedes and leathers for the company's West End Showroom – furnished in the height of modern taste and located in Great Marlborough Street.

His skill in tailoring PVC and plastics was channelled into 'Rainsport', a label specialising in outerwear and 'Leathersport', working exclusively in hide. A subsidiary company LMV Rainwear, with a factory in Manchester, was created to produce the brands.

In May John opened 'Capricorn', a company to specialise in luxury coats and suits, which enabled him to work in materials like suede and leather, and to sell at a more expensive level than Jean Varon and his other labels, targeting the same clients that shopped at Baccarat. The designs were long and sophisticated, with a military feel which complemented the high necked, nostalgic day and evening dresses which were becoming popular. 'Before I left Baccarat I explained to Monty Black that I was about to open Capricorn and therefore couldn't design both collections. To take my place I strongly recommended a young designer whose work I had seen in New York at that year's Yardley Award competition, which I had co-judged. I thought he should have won but was out-voted by my fellow judges. Monty was uncertain about this unknown designer but I eventually persuaded him to take him on'. The designer was Bill Gibb.

By the summer of 1969 John's designs were appearing in the fashion press under five different labels, and a decade of relentless promotion meant the profile of Jean Varon was at a high, exporting to forty-four countries across the globe and with twenty-eight boutiques in the leading stores across the country.

Opposite page
Maxi cape in black wool, yoked and deep hemmed in black, camel and white checks, rouleau tied at the neck. Beneath: a maxi skirt in the same checks, hemmed in black. John Bates for Capricorn. £37 10s.
Fashion Museum, Bath

Midi suit in burgundy jersey, the long jacket high collared, high vented; pockets, cuffs and belt tied through gilt eyelets. £44 9s. John Bates for Capricorn.
Fashion Museum, Bath

Producing and marketing a collection

6

Above John in his new Noel Street offices, the wall a testament to his success, circa 1967.
John Bates

John Siggins with an American fashion buyer at Noel Street.
John Bates

To produce so many designs for a variety of companies took planning – collections had to be shown to press, buyers and store manageresses and photographed for promotion. Production had to be co-ordinated to ensure that the clothes were streamed into the boutiques at the right time and delivered on the nail from the extensive network of manufacturers which Jean Varon now used.

For John, a collection began with the fabric, sourced from the trade shows every season in Germany, France, Italy and the UK.

'By the time the sample lengths came through, which was quite a while, I'd have to check with the supplier that they hadn't also sold the same pattern to anyone else. They, of course, would say no – but I'd find that they had sampled the same design to another firm. If another designer used the same fabric, our customers were very quick to let us know. Short-sighted of the fabric supplier maybe, but you can't blame them, for from their point of view there was no guarantee the sampling led to bulk orders of fabric.'

'When the fabric arrived I had it all unwrapped and stacked in my office so that I could see what I had bought months earlier and start thinking about what I was going to do with it. I think better by endlessly sketching ideas and it always takes about 300 sketches before a coherent look emerges, usually done lying on the floor. I had to bear in mind the typical Jean Varon customer if there was such a person – they weren't all film stars. A secretary say, who needed to buy a dress a week wanted something practical or pretty that didn't cost the earth. We hit that particular market pretty well I think, lots of Debs, secretaries, business women and of course actresses.

'Sometimes I'd make up for a collection and get so far through and hate it. I'd look at it and think "God that's not going to work – it's so much trouble". I'd have six fittings for something cut on the cross or a drape or those cut-outs – they look so easy but they're not. When it took too long it was either pushed to one side or I'd come back to it.

'I had to make sure the collection was balanced enough to supply all needs from day time, early evening and late evening, plus price structures. I would never sit down and think "Right I'm going to do a £9 dress" – I just designed it bearing in mind that there couldn't be a lot of work or a lot of cutting but still having a discernible look.

'We showed in April for the Winter Collection for delivery after the July sales, then a mid-season collection in June for Christmas, in September for Spring/Summer the following

year (which would be delivered after the January sales) and then another in February to perk up what was on offer that summer.'

The newspapers loved the designs for their theatrical innovation, and editors of magazines from *Nova* to *The Lady* knew that a Jean Varon collection would contain something to suit their readers. One of the keys of the success of the marketing was the forward thinking approach to photographing the clothes and distributing high quality images to editors using house models employed full-time at Noel Street.

'We would photograph things and instead of waiting for people to come in we'd send out a group of photographs with everything that was going on for the season to all the papers. Because they didn't have the money to do photographs or use model girls properly, or to set the whole thing up, they used them.'

For John the fabric came first, and he avoided cutting across patterns wherever possible; his designs became wearable works of art, with these sketches noting the use of four yards of fabric in each of the skirts.
John Bates

Lucy Bridgwater, great granddaughter of Lily Langtry, models a full length leather trimmed check coat and trousers by Capricorn, shot for *Harpers* in January 1970.
Sandra Lousada/National Magazines

The 1970s brought with them some of the most memorable, luxurious and financially successful of John's designs but also the shock of the early death of Eric West, one of the original backers of Jean Varon.

It forced both the future financial and design success of Jean Varon firmly on to John's shoulders, as managing director and sole designer, but also allowed a freedom in decision-making, enabling him to adapt the Noel Street showrooms to his own specifications in an ultra-modern style and to continue to expand his winning team of house models, manageresses and network of stockists, with small concessions within the department stores gradually expanding to form 'Shop in Shops'. These were to become one of the cornerstones of the success of the Jean Varon label in particular and eventually enabled the brand to be efficiently distributed nationwide.

John Siggins recalls 'We were in with House of Fraser, so that meant DH Evans, Dickins & Jones, Barkers, Derry & Toms – you got into one and you tended to spread around the other stores in the group.'

The size of stores varied, but as a development of the idea of a 'total look' Jean Varon designs could be sold together, with a much wider range than in smaller independent boutiques. 'Outside London the most successful was Rackham's of Birmingham, but then we had a very dynamic manageress there – it so often depended on the staff. Our manageress in Derry & Toms used to have a list of good customers, and would take the clothes to them.'

John Siggins would visit each 'Shop in Shop' in the UK every few months to keep up to date with customer feedback and to deal with any problems as they arose, constructing a highly developed distribution network. It also enabled the company to be aware of seasonal buying patterns often surrounding specific functions. 'You knew when a BMA dinner was coming up – there'd be a rush in a certain area – or the Caledonian Ball in Scotland – one manageress kept a list of what her other clients had bought to make sure there were no embarrassments of customers turning up in the same dress.

'In some respects having 'Shop in Shops' was a two-edged sword as some boutiques wouldn't buy if they knew a local department stored carried a larger range with more colourways. What they did give us was a continuity of orders – if you were dependent on independent retailers there was no guarantee that they were going to come back the following season. One minute you'd be chasing them for money, the next asking them to come and see the new collection.

'I used to have the regional manageresses down to London every season – we'd show them the collection and I would take notes on what they'd said, and we'd sit down and place orders for each location. You could interchange things between stores and all our staff tended to get on with each other. It gave us a very realistic assessment of our market – for example we did quite a healthy business in bridesmaid dresses, and there were certain styles you'd know would sell to that market – so we made sure we had pairs in 12s and 14s in whatever the pastel colour was that season.'

John with designs for Cilla Black
on the wall at Noel Street, circa 1967.
John Bates

91

History returns
to fashion

If the latter half of the 1960s had been about rising hemlines, the new decade saw a marked change in mood incorporating influences as disparate as romantic nostalgia, whether it be for smocked floral prints, or the 'Puritan' look of high collars and low hemlines, to new low cut bustlines, open-backed dresses and trousers worn under layers for day and evening.

The first changes picked up by the press came with the romantic teaming of printed dresses in cottons and chiffons with trousers – wide and straight or full and gathered below the knee. *Vogue* showed an example of the latter in October 1969 featuring a chiffon-smocked mini dress in green and white floral print with satin ribbon sash, over wide diaphanous trousers. The new romantic mood was also evident in the styling of the shoot; the setting was a woodland glade, and the model had tumbling pre-Raphaelite curls with soft, delicate features.

In November Prudence Glynn at *The Times* featured an example showing nine inches of trouser below a 'mixi' (neither mini or maxi) dress with smocked waist and paisley print, instilling a romantic Regency feel to the design. She eloquently summarised the mood – 'John Bates at Jean Varon has two lines evolving, both of which will be a major influence in the future. Firstly he has a series of dresses which realise fullness at different levels over a slim basic silhouette. For example, in one style the fabric flips out at bolero height, in the next it is held tight to the waist then released in a peplum, then a series of folds, over trousers. This is the second of his major themes and he repeats it in his collection of coats and suits at Capricorn.'

The new femininity also impressed Ernestine Carter in the same month for *The Sunday Times*. 'John Bates at Jean Varon has always alternated his moods of far-outness (the longest maxis or the shortest minis) with clothes that are just plain pretty, but pretty in his own vernacular.'

Part of Jean Varon's success as a label in the 1960s was an ability to run different looks together in a collection to cover a wider audience and there was no need to change this ethic as the new decade began. For every pretty, nostalgic dress reaching the pages of magazines there was a sleek, daring alternative waiting in the wings.

The first outfit by John to feature in *Vogue* for 1970 emphasised the dichotomy: a chamois suede boiler suit 'laced everywhere' with short sleeves and no back, available to order from Jean Varon at Chanelle boutique in Knightsbridge. In both material and design it was challenging, fresh and forward thinking. 'We sent the sample to Chanelle for the window and it was so

successful, it was shoplifted. One of Varon's best customers at Chanelle was a lady in her eighties who bought the shortest minis and anything in PVC. Unfortunately she was hit by a bus whilst wearing a black and white Varon PVC raincoat.'

Working with fine suede, wool, leather and fur at Capricorn, John was able to gain a new reputation for his distinctive use of fabric in his sleek coats shown in *Queen* in Autumn 1969; elegant and long in suede, or belted in wool with fox fur collars, or in military style, edged with leather for 1970.

'When I started a collection the inspiration had to come from the fabrics on offer for that season. I went to all the important fabric shows in Germany, Italy and France and selected what particularly appealed to me, whether extremely inventive and new, beautifully printed or just a plain fabric in a colour that caught the eye. I've always had favourite fabrics, usually plain like wool crepe, French jersey, organza, crepe de chines, voile and cotton. I would take swatches of the fabric ordered and on my return to London would pin them to the wall of my studio to digest the new designs and colours. The most difficult fabrics to design for are those printed as panels. Cutting through the design for me was not an option – that would destroy the very reason I had bought the fabric in the first place. This resulted in many hours spent pinning and draping the fabric on a stand to see what effect I could achieve without cutting through the panel. This could be both frustrating and exciting.

'Strong and Fisher were the first to develop a very soft complete cow hide which made it possible to construct coats, suits and dresses without the myriad seams which hitherto had been the norm for leather garments.'

Fashion editors now frequently reviewed John's designs for his different labels in the same article. Even though the customer base across the businesses was a broad one, a coherent style was always evident, with ideas being developed in different ways and fabrics across the range of prices.

Deirdre McSharry writing for *The Sun* in February 1970 commented on a new ideal figure 'Twiggy types are out – Raquel shapes are in', referring to the curvaceous new film star Raquel Welch, and went on to ask John about his new collections. 'Girls have got to learn to accept a new shape and to show more skin than they are used to' referring to his 'peplum and plunge dresses' bringing a new emphasis to the waistband accentuated by broad belts to many of the designs. *Vogue* in March featured a peplum dress with low cut neckline in 'navy linen with a frill peplum over the hips, tightly belted in navy patent' at twelve pounds, five shillings. New for 1970 was what *The Sunday Times* called the 'Primavera' look, referring to Botticelli's masterpiece depicting the arrival of spring. For March it picked a dress by Jean Varon in gold-brown celon chiffon printed in a random pattern of broken spots to illustrate the look, describing the sleeves 'floating from gathered tops, the skirt caught under the bosom and again at the hips'. For its use of bold print on chiffon the dress was a precursor of one of the most enduring looks of the 1970s for Jean Varon.

Since his early use of PVC and unusual fabrics sourced in Soho John was always happy to work with fabric producers and the early 1970s saw a rush of new names, with Jean Varon dresses often featuring in the promotions for the various firms involved. Names included Courtaulds' Tricel Surah, which was to be used extensively by John in the mid-1970s, Diolen and Trevira.

David Bailey photographed a dramatic tiered chiffon 'print and print, layer and layer' evening dress for *Vogue* in May, worn with

ribboned sandals from the Chelsea Cobbler and shot with a hint of the orient surrounded by inlaid damascus tables and brocade. By May a promotion of American cottons by Galey and Lord saw Clive Arrowsmith picture John's gypsy-inspired striped dress in 'Indian ink colours, arrowing up to a patent leather neck, laced in tasselled silk cords', the hem and cuffs edged with a deep band of lace.

Janet Street Porter's headline in the *Daily Mail* in August said it all 'Mini, Maxi, Now the Medi', referring to the medieval look in full-length evening dresses, illustrating the article with a Jean Varon dress in pale pink nylon organza with high waist, square neck and smocked sleeves, trimmed with gold appliqué braid – the model's hair plaited and styled like Queen Guinevere. Nyree Dawn Porter, appearing on television in *The Forsyte Saga* at the time, modelled a Jean Varon dress in the *Daily Express* in August; high-necked and with smocking across the bodice and cuffs.

Fashion's parameters had undergone a sea change in favour of the historical, whether it be romantic nineteenth century references, the tight sleeves and flowing skirts of an imagined medieval heroine or the 'Puritan' look, which was to provide Jean Varon with one of its best-ever selling dresses. John had the ability to adapt his designs for any one of his labels: for Jean Varon he produced romantic evening dresses with huge collars finished with pendant tassels, as modelled by Britt Ekland in *Vogue* in November 1970 and described as a 'jester' dress; for Capricorn, outfits featuring cloaks, opulent military inspired coats and layered tabards over trousers in the finest fabrics; and for Rainsport, bold maxi length raincoats, even tailoring PVC to produce a brilliant red skirt suit, promoted by *Rave* magazine as 'a very feminine way to keep dry' at nine guineas.

Ernestine Carter in *The Sunday Times* summarised the situation in October 1970 – 'John Bates is one of our designers who never picks up a fashion. He is with it at the start. His were and are the maxiest maxis, and he was ahead with the Midi long before Paris.'

Prints and Puritans

7

The early 1970s saw an explosion of vivid prints, whether it be Tootal's 'Aegean' print terylene voile featuring bold geometric designs used by Jean Varon in the spring of 1971, the vibrant Japanese-inspired floral satins in the autumn of the same year or the dotted and checked cottons of 1972. Not only were John's shapes as distinctive as ever, now the daring use of juxtaposing prints earned him a new reputation.

1971 was dominated by the 'Puritan' look, which gave John one of his most successful, and most widely copied designs. 'Knight' first appeared in *Vogue* in August 1971, photographed by Barry Lategan to simple and dramatic effect. In stitched Courtelle jersey the full length dress featured elbow length fitted sleeves and vertically seamed bodice and was worn over a silk blouse, described by *Vogue* as 'Worn like a pinafore over a beautiful plain Quaker collared white shirt with frilly wrists'. The design was enormously successful. The sharp tailoring emphasised the waist, the full skirt hid a multitude of sins, it was sophisticated, opulent and yet could be worn by a range of age groups. In its simplicity it left the high-necked Edwardian revival dress standing and paved the way for the layered pinafore dresses of the middle of the decade. 'The leggy London dolly bird has transformed into a long-gowned Venetian beauty' enthused the *Northern Echo,* with other designs from the collection named 'Byron', 'Quaker', 'Boleyn' and 'Seymour'. The look was also shown layered in grey wool with dramatic horizontal bands to the sleeves and to the two tiers of the skirt. The blouse beneath, like 'Knight', had deep frilled cuffs, but in this case the collar was raised like a ruff.

Always following in the wake of a successful design came copies from wholesale firms, who found a novel way of cutting costs. The richly pleated silk blouse, a vital part of the overall design of 'Knight', was a costly addition for firms trying to replicate the look but undercut on price, so copies soon appeared with the collars and cuffs sewn onto the body of the dress. As with most imitations of John's designs, the closer the inspection, the easier it was to tell the two apart.

The thriving middle market boutique scene, which had expanded throughout the country from the late 1960s onwards, together with more design-aware department stores, was largely due to the increased spending power of young women. Encouraged by magazines such as *Nova, Rave, Honey, Petticoat* and *Flair* they wanted access to the latest designs, and price was always a consideration in Jean Varon collections.

'If some unscrupulous competitors saw that we were quoted as having certain stockists in magazines they then used to approach them and try an undercut on price. One lot came a cropper when they tried to sell copies to the manageress of one of our "Shop in Shops", not realising she worked for us. She of course was straight on the phone to us. Unfortunately you couldn't get them for copying – all they had to do was change a stitch or detail and it was a different design – there was nothing you could do about it, but we did get them for "passing off".'

An Oriental journey

'Kimono sleeves' was *Vogue's* term for a hint of Japan making its way into the crepe de chine evening dress with plunging neck line featured in September 1971. It was John's alternative to the 'Puritan look'; sleek and simple, the detail was in the texture and fluidity of the fabric and the provocative neckline. *Flair* pictured the design centre page in its 'Japanese look' promotion the following month. 'Mikado' had wider sleeves still, in vibrantly printed Tricel Surah retailing at £19.25. The following year a boldly printed kimono dress combined an oriental shape adapted to feature a plunging neckline, in vivid floral print with a check border. As a flowing evening dress with wide cuffs and collars the design became 'Naiad', tying at the neck with drawstrings.

A twenty-four year old Helen Mirren wore Jean Varon's 'Moroccan' dress in metallic striped voile for *The Sun* in November 1971, photographed by Norman Eales. 'I like wearing costume, even in real life, this is a dress you have to act your way into' she said. Already gaining a reputation for her provocative roles, *The Sun* also shot her in another Jean Varon, this time white jersey and very low cut: 'I feel like a sex object in this – Women's Lib wouldn't approve.' Luckily, *Sun* readers did.

The djellabah was a perfect way of indulging John's love of dramatic print, and was a shape he was to interpret in a number of ways over the next few years. The ironically named 'McArab' combined the free flowing shape of a poncho in bold tartan with a white blouse with frilled tie cuffs and high collar in autumn 1971, and by 1972 the bold prints on Courtauld's Tricel Surah adapted the look to be worn by the pool, on the beach or as an alternative to a traditional evening dress.

Kimono style, low cut, fluid and simple;
featured in *Flair* in October 1970.
IPC Magazines

Right Fashion star, film star. John with 24 year old Helen Mirren, modelling a Jean Varon dress in a shoot for *The Sun*. *Norman Eales/The Sun*

Below left 'Naiad', named after the nymph of Greek mythology, retailed at £35.50, available at leading stores throughout the country in 1972. *John Bates/Selfridges*

Below middle 'Byron' in sheer Japanese printed voile; £19.75 from Marshall & Snelgrove of Oxford Street. *John Bates*

Below right Sculpted dresses in a Diolen fabric promotion in Vogue, 1971. *Diolen Ltd*

Fashion Contrasts and New Traditions

Opposite page
Top left Working with Austin Garrit enabled John to design in the finest fur, suede and leather, as seen in *Harpers & Queen* in 1973.
Saul Leiter/National Magazines

Top right House model Titch modelling 'Guardsman' for a Jean Varon publicity shot.
John Bates

Below Versatile day dresses with full 'bishop' sleeves and contrast overstitching became a hallmark of Jean Varon in the mid-1970s, this example retailing at £19.75.
IPC Magazines

The height of sophistication: John Bates for Austin Garrit, November 1972.
Andre Carrara/National Magazines

Checked, spotted or striped cotton layered dresses, whether plain or worn under a pinafore, became a Jean Varon triumph of the first half of the 1970s . Nobody did fuller skirts, or combined prints and colours in quite the same way. 'Pimento' had an Edwardian feel and layered skirts in tiny spots edged with stripes. Jean Shrimpton modelled it in *Vogue* on horseback in January 1972 and Judi Dench, heavily pregnant and firmly on the ground, wore a maternity version in *The Observer*. It heralded some of the most spectacular Jean Varon dresses of the decade. 'Carmelita' combined tiers of vivid checks edged in lace, in what the *Yorkshire Post* called 'Wild West Sweetheart' dresses, and it was not uncommon for fifteen yards of fabric to be used in the skirts alone. 'More colour, more fun… one thing over another' encouraged *Vogue* in March of Jean Varon's denim pinafore over of a version of 'Pimento', photographed by Clive Arrowsmith.

For autumn/winter the look was converted into luxurious fluid jerseys and wools shown at the autumn preview in April at The London Fashion Fair at the Grosvenor House Hotel. In a show entitled 'New Traditions' more than 100 designers previewed their collections for the season ahead.

Linda Millington of the *Birmingham Post* reported from the show and noted a new and subtle way of beating the copyists which had been such a problem with the design 'Knight'. 'Such blatant imitation will be more difficult with John Bates's latest collection, since the fluidity of line depends on the skilful cutting and quality of the cloth.'

Two silhouettes expressed the dramatic image created by John for the season. The first, a long swirling shape, almost like a coat dress, had a fitted bodice, tightly belted at the waist with neat yokes at the top, and full, full skirt. A version in bright red wool had collar, yoke, cuff and hem in black and white check. The second heralded the return of a new neater, shorter day dress, with all the style in the cut and decorative overstitching. 'Nikita' featured dropped shoulders, magyar sleeves and a gored skirt flared from the hip, with another version in grey with elbow length sleeves, shown worn over the same ruffled blouse as 'Knight'. Some fashion editors, referring to the hint of military smartness, called them 'Cossack dresses'.

Janet Street Porter for *The Evening Standard* in early September reported on their success – 'American buyers who flocked to see John Bates's collection breathed a sigh of relief – "Thank god someone is making superb day dresses"; for many it was the first collection they had seen in Europe featuring a dress you could actually wear to the office.'

Autumn/winter 1972 also marked a new collaboration with London-based furriers Austin Garrit. Already designing for the top of the middle market in coats and suits for Capricorn, the Austin Garrit Collection saw some of John's most luxurious designs to date in fur, suede and leather, and was a natural progression for his earlier work for Baccarat. He teamed soft suede with mink, matching sharply tailored suede trousers, with coats of curly Swakara trimmed with leather. For his sleeveless tabard suit, the sash belted tabard was worn over a beige suede blouse and matching trousers, the entire outfit retailing at £110.

Opposite page
Barry Lategan shoots Jean Varon's
'Wild West sweetheart' dresses for
Vogue in 1973.
*Barry Lategan/Vogue © The Condé
Nast Publications Ltd*

The body frocks
shock

In late October one of the most important fashion shows in London for years took place at Les Ambassadeurs club on Park Lane. For the first time the top four names in British fashion held their own joint show of designs for spring. John's collection joined those of Jean Muir, Zandra Rhodes and his close friend Bill Gibb, in front of selected British and foreign buyers and the international press. John Siggins recalls – 'Designers were complaining that nobody supported them… why didn't the Clothing Export Council, The Government, the fabric suppliers – anybody – underwrite shows for designers to participate in?' To be fair, the Clothing Export Council held breakfast shows to showcase designers' work at the beginning of Fashion Week, but there was no coordinated calendar for designer shows as there is these days. Export buyers were in town for such a short period it was impossible for them to cover all the individual showrooms in London.

'We decided to hold a combined show, each with our own autonomous section comprising twenty garments to give a flavour of the collection. We had our own model girls, our own music – the invitation list was a nightmare – fire regulations limited the number of people allowed in, and as is always the case many invitees did not reply, and some of those that did wanted to bring two or three guests. We had no idea who, or how many people would turn up. In the event buyers and press, both invited and uninvited, were queuing round the block to get in. Robert Mills, who with his mother Kitty owned Les Ambassadeurs, was seven feet tall and seven feet wide and stood in the doorway when the club was full blocking the entrance to all and sundry with American *Vogue* still stranded on the pavement – not for long though. Never have I felt more like a nightclub bouncer selecting the 'in' people from the queue; nobody else wanted to put their head above the parapet and risk upsetting an influential journalist or buyer so I had to. Inevitably one journalist, who hadn't RSVPed , turned up late and was refused entry, hated the show she hadn't seen!'

'They could have staged it 20 times over and still have standing room only', reported Barbara Griggs in the *Daily Mail* a few days later. Such collaboration between designers was rare in the UK and unheard of in France. Jean Varon showed black silk jersey dresses with huge batwing sleeves, and wide white stripes accentuating the inbuilt shape, vertical on the arms, horizontal across the waist. House model 'Titch' wore a black and white cotton blouse with circle skirt, the blouse with dolman sleeves, the skirt in gingham, accessorised with the increasingly popular pillbox hat with net veil.

However it was model Hazel's figure-hugging red crepe dress,

with matching hat and veil by Frederick Fox, that grabbed the headlines, and went on to feature heavily in the style magazines. *Over 21* featured the dress in November, picked by Fenwick's fashion buyer Jo Duncan, the company still buying from John a decade after its first orders for wedding dresses in the early 1960s. Conjuring up images of a 1940s film siren, it caught the imagination of journalists after several seasons of layers and body-concealing fashion. 'A real show stopper of a dress where the top is slashed so low and the skirt is cut so high there's almost nothing in between', commented Edwina Tarpley of the *Sheffield Morning Telegraph.*

Janet Street Porter, reporting on the new options for evenings in John's collections for the *Evening Standard* in early December 1972, called the new look the 'body frock'.

'From the front you may appear demure, even primly attired, a very different story lies around the corner, or over your shoulder. This year I predict another success for John Bates who has found what interesting effects a line of subtle ruching can have on the shape of your rear. His body frocks have full sleeves or draped fronts in slinky Banlon. In case you haven't got the message he slashes the hem up as far as decency allows'.

The dresses made it to the cover of *Cosmopolitan* in both December and the following January, featuring Julie Ege in 'yellow cleavage busting moss crepe'. The look was confident, provocative and yet still sophisticated, drawing on a nostalgic mood for glamour, very much in tune with the target *Cosmopolitan* audience. Dresses were now routinely teamed with tiny pill box hats by Frederick Fox, who was to work with John for the remainder of the decade.

Opposite page
With a man at her feet, Greta Morrison wears a pale blue evening dress cut to impress, perfectly suited to *Cosmopolitan*'s daring image in this shoot for the magazine in 1973. *Norman Eales/National Magazines*

January 1973: Julie Ege models a yellow crepe 'Cosmopolitan' dress, as requested by John Siggins from John each season to grab press attention. *Norman Eales/National Magazines*

Interviewed by the *Glasgow Herald* in mid January 1973 John explained how he went about introducing a new look into his collections. 'There are usually about 8 or 10 "testers" within my collections. Designs which are very different to the overall look of that collection. Some will look quite mad at first glance but will probably be the shapes that get developed for the next collection.'

Britain's impending entry into the European Economic Community in 1973 gave the London-based designers a new opportunity to tackle the European marketplace traditionally dominated by Paris, and one which was resistant to anything other than home grown talent. In the 'Fanfare for Europe' show, televised by the BBC from Lancaster House in London, Jean Varon designs joined Bill Gibb, Norman Hartnell, Ossie Clark and Barbara Hulanicki of Biba in an effort to promote British design. In February Prudence Glynn travelled with John as he opened his first Jean Varon shop in Europe within Illum department store in Copenhagen, and in April he went one step further with a ground breaking presentation in Paris. From the Musée de la Marine, he showcased the Jean Varon Autumn/Winter Collection', together with furs by Austin Garrit, shoes by Richard Smith at the Chelsea Cobbler and hats by Frederick Fox.

In his PR role John Siggins was responsible for European promotion through every available source. 'Immense support was given to British designers by Lady Henderson, the wife of the British diplomat Sir Nico, during his time as Ambassador to Poland, West Germany, France and the USA. No opportunity was missed by Mary to promote designers, and her hospitality was renowned'.

Sue Jarrett, John's showroom manager in London at the time, recalls the trip. 'The show very nearly didn't happen. The van with the collection broke down in France and John was already in Paris. The model girls, crew, dressers, hairdressers, music man and sound equipment were all flying out early on the day on a private flight, only just making it, as when we arrived at the airport there was no transport from the airport to the museum. All went well in the end and the show was a terrific success. Everyone flew back that night except for John Bates, John Siggins and myself, and we got caught in traffic later and missed our flight. We had to wait ages for another as they were all full with Fashion Week in London starting. I think I grew grey hairs over that trip, as we were due to show to buyers in the UK the following day.'

Opposite page
A Jean Varon backless sun dress in vibrant, heart-printed georgette with halterneck top guarantees attention in *Cosmopolitan*, Spring 1973.
Norman Eales/National Magazines

Above The 'body frock', clinging in all the right places for a film siren look, photographed for *Over 21* magazine, November 1972.
Over 21/Spotlight

John's designs from the early 1970s: short and tiered with underskirts of dotted net, or long and backless, caught with flowers and worn with veiled pill box hats.
John Bates

New layers for evening and the drama of the 'exit' line

Not every Jean Varon client had the figure to carry off a figure-hugging 'Cosmopolitan' dress as requested by John Siggins each season. An alternative for evening came in layered chiffon, pleated or plain, or vibrant printed Tricel Surah. David Bailey photographed one of the most elegant for *Vogue* in March 1973, the layers of cascading chiffon forming a waterfall of fabric, clinched at the neck and bust with flowers, by now a Jean Varon signature. The previous month international model Verushka photographed herself wearing a full length tiered 'nude chiffon' knife edge pleated dress in the *Sunday Telegraph Magazine*.

Above A perfect match for John's dramatic use of fabric, the Tricel Surah prints created some of the most memorable designs of the mid 1970s at Jean Varon.
Julian Allason/John Bates

Inspired by an aerial map of Luton and Braintree, the fabulous print designs of Sally McLoughlan for Jean Varon.
Julian Allason/John Bates

An alternative to the new chiffons were the ravishing prints by Sally McLoughlan for Courtaulds, with a range of her designs exclusive to John, on satin-like Tricel Surah. They included dramatic Art Deco geometrics, marbled effects inspired by the end-papers of a book, even a design based on an aerial map of Luton and Braintree. John's designs made sure the fabric was used to its full effect with dresses showing enormous sleeves, full circle skirts, knife edge pleating and tightly ruffled details, often edged in a black and white check to heighten the effect of colour and pattern colliding.

Prudence Glynn for *The Times* pronounced the Jean Varon show using the prints 'his best ever collection' in April, and the press promoted his extravagant evening blouse with huge tapering sleeves, the points almost touching the ground, over a frilled peplum, worn with black jersey trousers. Under the headline 'Labels that Mean London's World Leadership in Fashion' Terence Donovan shot the figures behind Jean Varon, Jean Muir, Bill Gibb, Mary Quant, Christopher McDonnell and Zandra Rhodes for *The Sunday Telegraph Magazine* in May. John appeared alongside John Siggins with model Kellie, she in a Sally McLoughlan print kaftan dress with tightly ruffled edges. The print was a riot of figures in an oriental garden inspired by a seventeenth century woodblock print, retailing at fifty-five pounds; there was a matching pillbox hat by Frederick Fox.

The backless full length dress 'Cosmos' in Banlon jersey heralded a new interest in the rear or 'exit line' of a dress. In this case, like the 'body dresses', the paring away was taken to its practical limits, with the base of the open back skimming the top of the buttocks, giving a reverse décolletée look. Needless to say it was this design that the press delighted in, but it also heralded a range of very wearable and dramatic designs for evening, with the exposed back framed by a frilled border, or covered in a sheer panel to match the remainder. Increasingly, the focal point of a dress reversed, or was picked out in embroidery and beading, whether it be a cobweb with tiny jet spider for a femme fatale look, or a full length, glittering sequined bird of paradise on a special limited edition jersey djellabah, retailing at £180 for autumn/winter.

Top Romantic layers of finely pleated chiffon in *Harpers & Queen*, April 1973.
Sandra Lousada/National Magazines

'Cosmos', cut lower at the back than any dress to date, meant that all eyes were on the artist, not her model, in this 1974 shoot for *Cosmopolitan*.
Bill Ling/National Magazines

The drama of the exit line: a backless dress circa 1971 shifts the emphasis of the design from entrance to exit. *Julian Allason/John Bates*

Contrasting designs for the mid 1970s:
sharp masculine tailoring, belted with
leather trim; for evenings, a luxurious
satin print blouse, the frilled cuffs almos
touching the ground, worn with wide
straight trousers; and the versatile
shirtwaister dress, which could be made
in almost any fabric to suit day or night.
John Bates

1974: John Bates – 'Almost couture ready-to-wear'

The continued success of Jean Varon ran seamlessly into the new season and 1974, with knickerbockers teamed with a halterneck top to grab the media's attention. As usual just the right level of body-conscious style teamed with attractive shots of a house model outside the Noel Street showrooms meant that the black and white images would appear in papers and magazines everywhere, whilst the remainder of the collection ensured the continued financial success. The new 'shirtwaister' shape for day and evening with high collars and buttons to the front could be worn by any age group and adapted to use almost any fabric, tied or belted at the waist in satin backed crepe or vibrant print, with box pleats to the skirt, or plain and full with ruffles at the collar.

David Bailey captured the new rainbow chiffon evening dress for *Vogue* in April, the floating skirts falling from a tiny bodice with fine shoulder straps, and 1930s styled fashion shoots paid homage to the film version of *The Great Gatsby* released that year. An alternative shape for day saw a sleeker, longer skirt and full bishop sleeves, which could be worn with a cloche hat and belted jacket to accentuate the nostalgia. Art Deco influenced prints made it to djellabahs and full, flowing evening dresses such as 'Tiddlewinks', a riot of spots and curves from the mid-season spring/summer collection.

The focus of the year was the opening of John's own name label available for autumn. His work for Baccarat, Capricorn and Austin Garrit had showcased the ease with which he designed for the luxury end of the ready-to-wear market. This proved beyond any doubt that he was just as adept at handling fine silk, suede and fur as the new manmade fabrics used extensively at Jean Varon.

Opposite page
Black worsted crepe, with silk birds and diamonds of rust and slate blue embroidered on the skirt, fitted yoked mandarin collared bodice, £420; hat by Frederick Fox.
Norman Parkinson Archive

The Best of British fashion: John Bates, Barbara Daly and Leonard add the finishing touches to model Kate Howard for Tyne Tees Television.
Clive Arrowsmith

It is a testament to the strength of his designs for Jean Varon that they were regularly shown alongside luxury ready-to-wear collections by Jean Muir, Bill Gibb and Zandra Rhodes. A close friend of Bill Gibb, he shared his love of embroidered suedes and leathers, luxuriant use of fabric, layers and repeated motifs. Both designers' very individual looks were to become based on craft and the ability to team juxtaposed prints, textures and materials in a commercially successful, innovative way.

The first collection, reported by all the major fashion editors, was a triumph. It included some of the most luxurious ready-to-wear clothes available in Britain at the time: long layered knits with matching mufflers, featherweight silk lined mohair coats, mink lined raincoats, feminine embroidered evening dresses in Liberty print wool, with pig skin detailing and JB motif belt buckles. Multi-thread coloured embroideries of birds of paradise, suede appliqués and contrast stitching featured heavily. One of the most distinctive pieces, a long black worsted coat dress for evening, embroidered in bands of birds in flight and geometrics, retailed at £420 and was photographed by Norman Parkinson for *Vogue* in September, with matching opossum muff.

'By this time Grace Coddington, who had modelled many of my clothes for *Vogue*, was now a senior fashion editor on the magazine and helped to promote my work in the most beautiful way'.

In an echo of the press coverage of 1965, Diana Rigg returned to model the new collection for the *Daily Express* in September, wearing a black Swakara evening suit trimmed with opossum and worn with toning silk blouse, the ensemble retailing at £1,250, later slipping into a burnished orange djellabah at £175. 'John was the first one to say to me: "Right you're tall. Smashing. You've got broad shoulders. Excellent. Let's see what we can make of it all"', she commented.

As the clothes became more exclusive, so did the stockists, including Fortnum & Mason, Selfridges and Harvey Nichols. In an unprecedented move a 'John Bates Boutique' opened in the International Room of Harrods, alongside designers such as Lanvin, Givenchy and Courrèges. Furnished in brown glass and chrome with fixtures and furniture in brown leather by Evelyn Etkind, the retail environment matched John's 'almost couture ready-to-wear' perfectly. This was shortly followed by an impressive Jean Varon shop within the Designer Room, both reflecting the décor of their respective showrooms.

Opposite and following pages
John's sketches for his own label, using the finest printed silks, suedes, fur and embroidery.
John Bates

Marie Helvin and Hazel Collins model luxury in Liberty wool and embroidered pigskin, with glittering JB initialled belt, from the first John Bates collection, 1974.
Mode Wohnen

John Bates. 74.

John Bates 74.
Black + White

Bianchini Black Silk. unlined

A 1" elastic inserted here?
make it fit over like this, but can be pulled off as sketched OK.

M.O.T. Wool

Appliqué in Pongees Silk

John Bates 74.

John Bates 74.

Silk Appliqué on to pure wool.

JOHN BATES.

BIANCHINI SILK.
SEE THROUGH BACK.

John Bates.
74.

John
Bates
'74

Pure Silk
Adrianno Stuehi.

John Bates
74.

John Bates 74

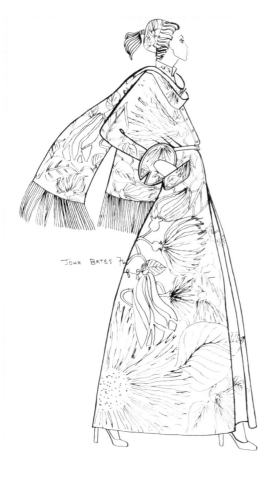

JOHN BATES 74

JOHN BATES 74

JOHN BATES 74.
ALL ONE COLOUR KNITTING.
VERY FINE AND LIGHT.

JOHN BATES
74.

BLACK WOOL
ENSEMBLE. COAT
BORDERED IN BLACK
DYED OPOSSUM.
DRESS EMB. AT
HEM IN SILK
THREAD TO
MATCH.

LEATHER TOP.

JOHN BATES
74.

SILK.

Style along parallel lines

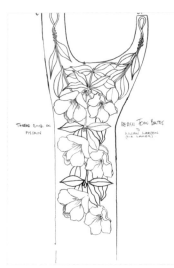

Opposite page
Navy and white silk chevron stripes, dolman sleeve duster coat sashed in fringes, with full skirt over a navy dirndl, £350; shot for *Vogue* in March 1975.
Oliviero Toscani/Vogue © The Condé Nast Publications Ltd

Top, left John Bates appliqué wool crepe shawl, skirt and blouse, £274 at Selfridges.
John Bates

Top, right Design for a sleeve embroidered on pigskin; one of John's most practical skills was the ability to hand-draw complex designs for embroidery.
John Bates

Below Appliquéd and embroidered djellabah, circa 1975.
Niall McInerney/John Bates

John was used to designing at contrasting ends of the marketplace, but with the Jean Varon and John Bates collections now running in parallel he was able to develop themes which ran between the two without ever duplicating looks.

One of the first drew inspiration from embroidered piano shawls with long fringing, and featured in both collections for 1974/75. For Jean Varon, a heavy black crepe evening dress with a plunging neckline, vaguely 1930s in feel, was finished with five inch deep fringing under the bust line and on the cuffs, swaying as the wearer moved. Elizabeth Morris for *The Scotsman* reported from the John Bates collections for spring 1975 – 'Handkerchief points on his crepe de chine dresses finished in a matching tassel, tassels were also suspended from sleeves and hung like bell pulls from the ends of stoles and shawls, and they made stylised stamens in silk flowers.' Dresses were now accessorised with beautifully embroidered long fringed shawls decorated with simple stylised floral motifs, or repeating the exotic bird of paradise.

The chiffon or georgette evening dress was rapidly becoming one of the best selling lines for Jean Varon, and the flared, tiered shape could be interpreted each season with a different neckline. The dramatic emphasis was varied with pendant tassels, ruffled edges or embroidery. The Jean Varon style 'Rogers', a pleated swirling chiffon evening dress with one shoulder, used over fifteen yards of fabric and the *Birmingham Post* in December celebrated 'a fine disregard for economy' in the Jean Varon collections, with pleats everywhere.

Exquisite detail in shape, fabric and form characterised the John Bates collections: for spring 1975, a black skirt and jacket trimmed with appliqué flowers from the mid-season collection, again modelled by Diana Rigg, was the epitome of subtle chic. The focus of the collection was a white wool wedding dress with panels of silk, embroidered and beaded, shown with tasselled collars and matching hat by Frederick Fox. From the same collection a honey-coloured silk evening dress was embroidered with gold thistles.

'When I wanted embroidery I used Steve Laker of Lillian Warton in Heddon Street, off Regent Street for everything. He allowed me to prepare everything myself, like drawing up the design exactly to fit whatever model was being made. This had to be very accurate and it took a long time to do – usually 2 days' work for me on special waxed paper. The next step was for them to perforate the design and transfer it onto the fabric by rubbing chalk through the perforations. I then selected all the beads and sequins to be used, making sure

Silken elegance
by John Bates
Dress and shawl by John Bates.
In an exclusive printed silk. Trimmed with
embroidered cape leather. Sizes 10 to 14
£260. Hat made specially to order.
Selfridges
DESIGN ROOM

Something
to make
a thong
about

John Bates
will be making a
personal appearance
in our International
Room on Wednesday
27th April at 11am
and 2.30pm to
present our
collection of his
inimitable creations.
No tickets required.

From the collection we
show a pigskin jerkin and
silk shirt in 'Deep Green'
teamed with
Black wool trousers.
8 to 14 £200
Personal shopper only

♕ ♕ ♕ **Harrods**

Top 'Silken Elegance', modelled by
Wendy: a John Bates advertisement
in *Vogue* teams silk with leather and
a picture hat, available from Selfridges
at £260.
John Bates/Selfridges

Promoting a personal appearance at
Harrods by the designer, a John Bates
design in pigskin, silk and wool, laced at
the vertical seams; £200 from Harrods.
Eric Stemp/John Bates

the colours complemented each other. If it was bead work,
the fabric was stretched very tightly over frames and then
embroidered from the reverse side. I've always had great
admiration for the skill of Mr Laker's technicians. If it was
appliqué or multi-thread work (as in any of the big djellabahs
I loved doing) very large pieces of fabric had to be managed
on a very heavy machine with no guards – just the needle
and the embroiderers' nimble finger movements. Very balletic
and terrifying to watch.'

For John Bates, wide-brimmed picture hats were made from, or
lined with, the same fabric as day dresses. These came in silk
with full sleeves and slimmer skirts, printed in chevrons or in
pretty florals, as photographed by Duffy for *Harpers and Queen*
in May 1975.

Jean Varon had coordinated dresses, scarves and hats in bold
geometric print, using the same fabric for each, retailing at
£62.95. As ever, when a design struck a particular chord with
buyers it appeared in a variety of media. 'Comet' in 'Courtelle'
jersey with white overstitching and integral cravat was a simple,
sophisticated day dress. David Bailey pictured it for for *Vogue*
in February 1975, and Cabinet Minister Barbara Castle was
photographed wearing it.

With such a variety of customers now looking to John for
inspiration each season, his dressmaking pattern promotions
offered many the chance to make and adapt his designs.
Woman magazine offered its readers 'A very grand dress but
easy to make' featuring a backless evening design with multi-
stitched collar, panelling to the bodice and full sleeves nipped
in at the cuff. The magazine enthused that it could be made up
in a number of fabrics, the pattern costing twenty-seven pence.
For those wanting something much more challenging, Prudence
Glynn in *The Times* offered readers the chance to make and
embroider their own version of John's bird of paradise djellabah,
suggesting the embroidery could be picked out in sequins as
with the original £180 version, or using appliqué fabric sections.
'I would have loved to have seen some of these finished efforts.'

Looking ahead to 1976 John told the *Draper's Record* in October,
'I see spring as a strict fluid look, tailored yet comfortable, in
natural fabrics such as combinations of linen and silk. I'm doing
a total look, complete with bags this time'. True to his word, for
spring the John Bates label even showed coordinated linings in
raincoats and umbrellas.

Barbara Griggs for the *Daily Mail* assessed the John Bates
collection, shown at The Berkeley Hotel in Knightsbridge: 'John

Bates cuts the purest line in London, a smooth soft flow from wrist to throat, with built in curve and shape' and pictured 'Cascade' in pure silk satin. The collection included a long knit suit with silk shirt, the jacket trimmed in fox fur and as a headline grabber, an oriental fantasy gown featuring hand painted silk panels, like panels on a Chinese vase, over a pleated underdress, available at stockists including Harrods at £450.

Diana Rigg modelled more from the collection for spring in the *Daily Express* in December 1975, as happy in John's luxury clothes as she had been in his designs for *The Avengers.* She chose a fluid crepe de chine evening dress printed with tulips, a swirling cream raincoat with matching skirt and blouse, and a black silk printed dress with matching scarf. Of her favourite designers she said 'For functional go-everywhere clothes that never date I go to Saint Laurent and sometimes Sonia Rykiel. But when I want something sexier, and more languorous, it's straight to Jane Cattlin and especially to John Bates'.

Top John Bates designs for 1975: 'Rogers' in swirling pleated chiffon for evening, and a trapeze cut black linen coat dress with coordinating umbrella. *John Bates*

Selling at the heart of fashionable London: the Jean Varon and John Bates boutiques within Harrods, exquisitely designed in chrome, glass and leather. *John Bates*

Rule Britannia – the international market

9

The logistics of showing both Jean Varon and John Bates collections to assembled buyers each season took some organising. John Bates showed at the Berkeley Hotel in front of a selected audience of around 300, with Jean Varon based in the Noel Street showrooms.

John Siggins recalls buyers visiting Noel Street: 'We should have had three shows a day but people were often late – so we showed continuously like the Windmill Theatre in Soho – the girls came in, and they'd finish one show and there'd be customers there who had missed the beginning, so it was a rolling thing. We served elevenses – tea and sandwiches. One of our seasonal dressers was so punch drunk after a full day unzipping model girls, when travelling home on the underground she unzipped an unsuspecting girl who turned her back on her.'

'Export collections would be determined by the exhibitions. Sometimes they would be early, sometimes late. We would know that we had to have an export collection ready to go to the exhibition in say Dusseldorf or Paris before we showed in London.'

Foreign buyers visiting London for the shows had strict limits on the amount of time spent looking at individual designer's collections before jetting off to the next European city on the their list 'If you look at it dispassionately the amount of time and space that you gave them when they came to London really wasn't reflected in the orders that they placed. But it was very good to have a name like Neiman Marcus, Saks Fifth Avenue or Bergdorf Goodman as a stockist as it brought other people in. It opened the door for us to eventually have a showroom in New York.'

British fashion as a force in the international marketplace was highlighted in a special television show of the 'Best of British' from Chatsworth in Derbyshire in March 1976, compered by actor Anthony Valentine and organised by Prudence Glynn. She commented 'We import far too many clothes and our textile industry is in an appalling state. If we don't recognise this and do something about it we will lose them – and that would be the end of us.'

She was voicing concerns of many in the industry that Britain's fashion profile abroad had lost the dynamism it was renowned for in the Sixties, with innovation and professionalism left to an increasingly small number of designers such as John.

Ironically international sales for Jean Varon were some of the strongest ever, helped by the widely promoted Pompeii

collection, designed to coincide with the exhibition at the Royal Academy in London in the autumn of 1976. In conjunction with ICI fabrics John designed a small group of dresses inspired by ancient Rome in draped terylene jersey, ready to be in the shops for the opening of the exhibition in November. With design names such as 'Thisbe' and 'Ariadne' the clothes were beautifully simple, relying on the skilful draping and the fluidity of the fabric. It was to be one of the most promoted collections for Jean Varon of the period, helped by images such as those shot by James Wedge for *The Sunday Times Magazine* in November, and by John's headline-grabbing topless evening dress.

'The eruption of Vesuvius could hardly have caused more of a stir than this topless dress that burst into ICI's showroom' wrote Suzy Menkes for the *Evening Standard.* 'Britomaris' was modelled by Lavina and prompted one regional paper to suggest that perhaps it was 'a fireside dress rather than for going out on the town.' True to form the tabloids loved it and arranged for their own models to feature the dress. John Siggins: 'The dress was a showcase dress and not seriously meant for anyone to wear, in fact it had so little fabric in it that it was difficult to cost and the outworker was so sure we wouldn't sell it, he even offered to make it for nothing – a rare offer which we took him up on, much to his dismay when the orders came in. We did a particularly brisk trade in Harvey Nichols.'

Autumn/winter 1976 saw more wearable and relaxed designs from Jean Varon, including the tunic, belted as a day dress or worn over a skirt in prints by Bernard Nevill, and for evening a series of delicately embroidered dresses using rhinestones, named after famous jewellers. 'Bishop' in panels of wool crepe personified the versatile day dresses which were becoming as popular as his designs for evening wear. With full sleeves, the simple tunic with fitted buttoned yoke merged day and early evening.

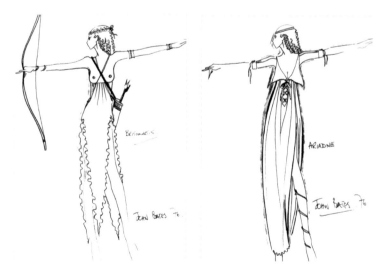

The new classicism: from the 'Pompeii'
collection, inspired by ancient Rome and
produced to coincide with the exhibition
at the Royal Academy in the autumn of
1976.
ICI fibres

For John Bates, a luxurious wool crepe djellabah, appliquéd in black silk, stitched in ultra violet thread and photographed for *Vogue* by Willie Christie, retailed at £634. A series of spectacular satin dresses for evening, soft and fluid, complemented sunray pleated evening trousers worn tied at the ankle. A look of Arabia filtered through the swirling fabrics, with harem trousers teamed with draped cloaks and head scarves. Prudence Glynn felt it John's best collection to date for the label.

For spring David Bailey shot Jerry Hall in an electric green flared short suede jacket with matching beret by Frederick Fox for John Bates, and Willie Christie worked his magic on a John Bates photo shoot for *Vogue*, photographing 'spinning pleat orange blossom evening dresses and floating flower satins'.

The success of both the John Bates and Jean Varon brands abroad was crowned with the opening of John's showroom at 550 Seventh Avenue in New York in the Jubilee year.

> 'Ben Shaw, a legendary fashion entrepreneur, approached John about representing the Varon and Bates collections in the United States. Seventh Avenue is the rag trade in New York and each of the skyscrapers had a different type of merchandise. 550 housed the luxury fashion houses, including Oscar de la Renta, Bill Blass and Richard Assatly. Buyers would come in from all over the States and spend the week visiting the designers in turn. They had a typical New York deli on the ground floor. The girl on the counter there knew more about the rag trade than anyone else. She'd know how much business people had done, who was "in" and who was "out"– and who was about to be fired – she'd have all the information!'

They would cover the marts in Dallas, Chicago and Los Angeles which, as in Britain, attracted buyers for stores throughout the country, but unlike the UK could be buying for as many as 400 outlets.

Copies were, as ever, a problem. 'They would knock you off – the minute a garment hit the rails in the stores a cheaper copy would be produced by someone. We used to get telephone calls from customers saying, "We didn't know you were in that store – how clever of you to use different labels."'

Opposite page
Understated, draped silk glamour by
John Bates, shot for *Vogue* to illustrate
an interview with the designer in 1976.
*Barry Lategan/Vogue © The Condé
Nast Publications Ltd*

Pared down elegance for 1976:
increasingly simple silhouettes in luxury
fabrics trimmed with leather, embroidery
or beading.
John Bates

Willie Christie shoots John's
sophisticated, feminine print day
dresses for *Vogue* in March 1977.
Willie Christie/Vogue © *The Condé
Nast Publications Ltd*

A leaner, sleeker silhouette

As fashion moved toward a slimmer, more masculine silhouette John established a new style vocabulary which was to see out the decade. The skilled draping of fabric became everything, both for the luxury fabrics of John Bates and with the crepes and jersey at Jean Varon. Tight Fortuny-like pleats gave a new look to the pared-down classical shapes first seen in the Pompeii collection, and at John Bates hip-hugging trousers were teamed with crepe de chine blouses and reversible capes or bomber jackets. The 'overall' dress was a simple tabard shape, could be belted in and suited almost any fabric treatment for day or early evening; in silks for John Bates or crepe for Jean Varon. John took his body-conscious style to the limit with his range of swimwear for summer, with a favourite model Hazel showing a tiny draped and tied bikini. The same collection brought a daring one-piece swimsuit, a pleated 'V' of fabric hugging the body with horizontal ties and a drape of fabric over the shoulders.

A pared-down simplicity began to flourish, and gained more column inches when the same daring halter necks from the swimwear collections were translated into satin for evening. These were teamed with satin evening 'jodhpur' trousers tailored with narrow legs and folds of fabric at the top, and worn with fine floating jackets in silk or lace. Willie Christie again caught the moment for *Vogue*, and by autumn fly-collared shirts worn with ties and trousers fitted to the ankle, tail coats and wool trousers trimmed with suede were added to the collection for John Bates. The evening dresses were slim and sophisticated, one described as a 'pillar of black satin' with a deep 'V' at the back, the fabric draped to form a peplum over a full skirt as modelled by Hazel for *The Tatler* in November. On her shoulder was a brooch containing 20.5 carats of diamonds.

The list of John's clients at John Bates was by now impressive. Returning customer Diana Rigg was joined by Cleo Laine, Sian Phillips, Elaine Stritch and Hilary Tindall, and members of the Royal Family were regular wearers. Twiggy was even persuaded to model again for an editorial shoot for *The Observer* in December, who had asked Bill Gibb and John to create clothes using fake fur. John's design of an imitation fitch cape was shown over leather embroidered trousers with matching fur trim, as the paper highlighted the growing opposition to the use of fur which had always been a traditional part of the luxury fashion world.

Jean Varon's following was by no means depleted, as continued inclusion in women's magazines and the regional press kept the brand at the forefront of the market in which it had always thrived. *The Edinburgh Evening News* asked its readers to name the best occasion to wear each of four pictured Jean Varon dresses, the options including 'Going to the Opera', 'A Garden Fete' and

Top Champions of export at the British Embassy in Paris: Bill Gibb, Sir Nico and Lady Mary Henderson and John Bates. *John Bates*

Below, left Pure glamour from John Bates: a single shouldered evening dress for autumn/winter '77/'78. *John Bates*

Below, right John's talent for designing body conscious clothes translated easily to swimwear; shot for *The Times* in 1978. *Peter Akehurst/The Times*

Opening Today

John Bates
London

Appointment 550 Seventh Avenue, New York. Telephone (212) 398 9000

'Dinner Dance'. The prize was a Jean Varon dress up to the value of £100. In the same month *Good Housekeeping* pictured John behind his faultlessly composed Christmas dinner party table with ceramics by Wedgwood, for their 'Ideal Setting' feature, adding to the growing interest in the individuals behind popular brands.

Fashion shows by regional department stores, charity dinners and the social pages of a host of magazines always included a sprinkling of Jean Varon dresses and journalists for the majority of local papers would regularly comment on the latest collections from London. By the end of 1977 John's designs were being sold from the new showroom in New York and across the States. In the UK, cutting edge individual boutiques like Lucienne Phillips and Chic of Hampstead, and luxury department stores stocked the John Bates label, with the 'Shop in Shops' and regional boutiques selling Jean Varon. It had never been easier to find a John Bates design, anywhere in the world.

Top Announcing the arrival of John Bates in New York, an advertisement for the opening of the American showrooms at 550 Seventh Avenue.
Angela Landells/John Bates

Left The designer at home: John poses in his London dining room with his 'Ideal Setting' for *Good Housekeeping*, ceramics by Wedgwood.
John Cook/National Magazines

Above At the Savoy: John Bates, sales director Sue Jarrett and John Siggins.
John Bates

Above Evening dress in soft silk chiffon
with a smattering of velvet snowflakes,
£480 from the John Bates Boutique at
Harrods.
Eric Stemp/John Bates

John Bates designs for 1978: sharp
tailored shapes, fluid fabrics and swirls
of pleats.
John Bates

JoHn Bates.
77. for 78.

JoHn
Bates. 77.

JoHn Bates.
77 for 78.

Embroidered blue suede tail coat over
silk shirt and black wool trousers
edged in suede.

JoHn Bates.
FoR 78.

Down to the bare essentials

Opposite page
Tightly tailored for 1979: 'Squeak', with
double breasted jacket, nipped-in waist
and pill box hat.
Richard Dormer/John Bates

'Romance' for Jean Varon in multi-
stitched chiffon, the frilled collar centred
by a whirl of flowers, modelled by Wendy
Howland.
Richard Dormer/John Bates

'Dare you bare for the Cleopatra look?' asked the *Yorkshire Post* in April 1978, referring to a column of jersey, ruched vertically to the centre on spaghetti straps and christened 'Cleopatra' by John, 'draping and touching where it matters' according to the paper. Of course the answer was 'yes', as fashion left the 1970s looking lean, uncluttered and formal, with a nod to the silver screen glamour of the 1940s.

As Britain moved towards a severe recession several designers were beginning to find it difficult to continue in the luxury market, not least Bill Gibb who had been let down by a number of backers and was forced to stop showing periodically. John's business base was wider and he was thus able to gain greater protection in a leaner UK marketplace.

Ironically a tougher economic environment brought even more luxurious clothes. John's hallmarks, including the sumptuous use of fabric, were translated into short flowing cloaks worn with trousers over a smocked jacket in 'Sleuth', and a long pheasant feather worn on a hat, or used to centre a ruffle of fabric, became as good as a John Bates label as far as fashion commentators were concerned.

Mandarin collars gave button-through rayon overall dresses in pretty prints a sleek new look, and the wrap dress for day and evening gave John the chance to combine eroticism with chic once again. Evening dresses were cut low to the waistband and slashed to the thigh, the waist emphasised by silk cummerbunds or oriental inspired ties. The scarf dress 'revealed and concealed'. For Jean Varon, 'Perhaps' used metallic woven voiles, layer on layer in gold on black, with a new three-quarter-length jacket, semi-sheer with a simple drawstring collar. This was worn with ankle-length full skirts or over slim trousers to showcase the fabric.

In August 1978 *The Tatler* gave the John Bates collection five out of five stars: 'A large collection full of opulent luxurious clothes, as good for wearable daytime suits, dresses and coats as for his night time extravaganzas. His powerful cut is accentuated by stark black and vibrant red, and at night he combines cream lace and silver brocade in a manner that is irresistible. Leathers look butter soft, reversible cloaks are swagger smart and wool crepe dresses unbuttoning to show cord knee breeches, are a surprising delight.'

'Romance' in multi-stitched chiffon proved there was still a place for floating, pretty evening dresses in the collections, the frilled collar centred by a whirl of silk flowers. 'Myopic' hit the other end of the scale, a sheer evening dress with the neckline dipped to

the waist, the full sleeves, and bodice trimmed in satin, the layered chiffon skirt slit to the thigh, finished with a satin sash tie.

'Gladys' burst onto the scene late in 1978 during an Indian summer. In gold sequins, the bra top and shorts with matching hat cost £50 from Jean Varon – 'perfect for beachcombing or disco dancing' enthused Jackie Modlinger at the *Daily Express* in October. The tabloid press approved for the usual reasons. For the party season, an increasingly supportive Anne Price at *Country Life* commissioned Richard Dormer to shoot another sparkling Jean Varon outfit, this time a silver lurex pleated 'bubble' dress, in a shape which was to become synonymous with the '80s, available at £64.

'John Bates's ideal woman is a vamp, but she won't scare the living daylights out of you – she's a sexy siren who gets down to the bare essentials', wrote the *Newcastle Evening Chronicle* in January 1979.

For spring John showed short, tailored and belted jackets with draped skirts and wrap dresses in Italian print silks, crepe de chines and satins, in muted colours with flashes of scarlet, bright yellow and the model's thigh.

New for 1979: full taffeta skirts for
evening, worn with tailored satin
jackets; sleek, draped column dresses
with lamé bodices and jackets.
John Bates

The John Bates label designs were never more body-conscious or dramatic, and only five years after its opening the fashion landscape was almost unrecognisable. Evening dresses were dramatically cut away, revealing panels meeting at the waistline and draped to hug the legs, exotic trousers suits were worn with exquisite, luxurious fabric jackets or hand screen-printed chiffon panels. For day, suits were trimmed with fur and sharply tailored, trousers were worn fitted, with elegant soft leather coats and capes, one black leather trapeze-cut coat embroidered with birds in silk along the hem.

Jean Varon existed, as ever, in tandem, and translated the luxury fabrics into more affordable crepe de chines, rayon and georgette. Sequins glittered on the bodice of a dress or as a trim on evening capes in chiffon. Dresses still used metres of fabric to make sure that any copy by competitors was never able to grasp the look of a John Bates design. For what was essentially a middle market designer company, the Jean Varon dresses of this period interpreted the glamour of the John Bates line remarkably closely, with one black jersey draped column evening dress matched with a black sequin jacket, trimmed with a huge ruff of feathers, and tied with a satin ribbon. It was unadulterated glamour, and Jean Varon made it available from a department store.

One of the best, Simpson's of Piccadilly, displayed the cream of British fashion for autumn 1979, and so impressed were the organisers that they approached each of the designers involved in turn to discuss the feasibility of donating their dress to the Victoria & Albert Museum, together with the Rootstein mannequin used by the store. John Bates provided a black jersey evening dress, draped and cut away at the waist, one side of the skirt ending with a beaded tassel attached at the wrist and worn with a tiny feathered cocktail hat by Frederick Fox. The dress joined examples by Jean Muir, Bill Gibb, Zandra Rhodes and Yuki as a 'snapshot of fashion' in the museum collection.

Photographer John Swannell instinctively captured the erotic charge of John's designs of the late 1970s, increasingly using metallic fabrics, sequins and including daring wrap dresses in silk and satin.
John Swannell

Autumn 1979 also saw John's first menswear collection for his own name label, showing complementing male and female versions of the same outfits, using suede and leather on tweed. Jackets were three-quarter length with squared shoulders, or short bomber jackets, accessorised with matching hats, ties and belts, and made by his friend Monty Black of Baccarat. Reid and Taylor who were producers of the finest and most expensive wool cloths for suits, commissioned John, Bill Gibb, Tommy Nutter and Yuki amongst others to design a range of menswear to be showcased at Leeds Castle in front of 800 guests including Princess Margaret. *Harpers and Queen* featured one of John's designs for an asymmetrically buttoned silk shirt, short jacket and buttoned trousers in September the same year and Anthony Crickmay photographed both John and Bill Gibb in their own designs.

Three designs caught the attention of the press for that autumn. 'Ingot' a sequined jacket, bra top and fitted trousers, was worn with a tiny feather trimmed hat by Frederick Fox, as was 'Carat' with complementing short jacket over jodhpur-style trousers. The reason for the attention: both came in metallic gold from top to toe. The third, a design for Phillip Hockley, meant that press coverage for the year ended on a high – for total luxury, a floor-length silver-tipped fox-trimmed black leather coat, with panels of thread embroidery and hand beadwork, retailed at a headline-grabbing £5,082.

Opposite page
From the 1979 John Bates catwalk: jodhpur trousers with the briefest silk halternecks, overstitched tailored crepe day dresses with sharply fitted shoulders, and a fox fur trimmed embroidered leather coat – 'almost couture ready to wear'.
Niall McInerney

Left, above 1979 saw John's first collection of menswear: shot for *Harpers & Queen* in September, a matching jacket, shirt and trousers with asymmetrical button details.
National Magazines

Left, below Menswear publicity shots by John Swannell with leather, satin and sheer panels adding a spark to John's designs for a sector still dominated by traditional looks.
John Swannell

Already a wearer of his designs, Princess Margaret chats to John at Leeds Castle, with ever-present cigarette, Autumn 1979.
John Bates

Into the limelight: John's inherent sense of style translated easily on to stage and screen – sketches for Jenny Runacre in *The Final Programme*, Sian Phillips as Vera in *Pal Joey*, Elaine Stritch in *The Fatal Weakness* and Cleo Laine in the *Cleo Laine Spectacular*.
John Bates

Just how diverse a marketplace existed for John's designs was neatly summarised in 1979 with the release of Neil Simon's film *California Suite*. Not only did Maggie Smith wear a Jean Varon chiffon evening dress for most of the film, playing opposite Michael Caine as an Oscar nominee awaiting the result, but Princess Margaret wore a chiffon and ribbon trimmed Jean Varon dress to the Royal Film Performance itself in March.

John Siggins recalls the lifestyle: 'The 1970s became increasingly hectic, fabric fairs, trade fairs in Paris, Milan, Munich and New York whilst still showing in the London showroom, and promotional trips to the United States filled the year. Supper most nights at San Lorenzo and then back to work, though sometimes a working supper for two increased during the evening to one of six or eight, as other designers or writers joined the table.'

San Lorenzo, owned by Mara and Lorenzo Berni in Knightsbridge, was a meeting place for designers, writers and stylists, and a safe haven for film actors to eat in peace without the intrusion of fans. John Bates loved it so much that Mara and Lorenzo closed the restaurant for his 'after-show' parties each season.

As the business expanded it became economical to make extra stock for the showroom, which retailers visited during the season to replenish their rails. It also became the first port of call for stylists looking for clothes for television shows and commercials, as well as various Bond girls and beauty queen contestants. 'One of our best clients was a night club singer who bought evening dresses for his dancers – he did more business with us than some of the smaller out of town shops.'

Offers to design for theatre, television and film were abundant but, unless the production could be dressed from stock, were not always possible to take up – especially for film and television, where time is of the essence. 'We were first and foremost a fashion house and it was not feasible to take machinists off making a collection because a film unit needed a dress in a hurry when the shooting schedule had changed.' Theatre was much more civilised, though John's introduction to costume design was less so.

Whilst working at Herbert Sidon he had been allowed to design one dress for Joan Heal in a production of *Grab Me a Gondola*. The design consisted of a figure-hugging dress with two hands embroidered over the bust. John embroidered the dress himself and, satisfied that it looked good, sent it off to the theatre for the dress rehearsal. Herbert Sidon took John to the rehearsal and when the moment arrived for his dress to make an entrance, the

embroidery could not be seen from the front row of the circle, which of course Sidon knew would be the case. John worked through the night to change the embroidery for the next day's opening, with huge chunks of glass replacing the chic crystals and sequins. It worked, and the dress got its laugh.

Stage, screen and television credits

Theatre
Grab Me a Gondola – Joan Heal
Pal Joey – Sian Phillips
Passion Play – Judy Parfitt and female cast
Coupe de Soleil – Sian Phillips
Dear Liar – Sian Phillips
Anthony and Cleopatra – Judy Parfitt
Blues in the Night – Cast
The Fatal Weakness – Elaine Stritch
So what about Love – Sheila Hancock
Verdict – Hilary Tindall

Film
The Final Programme – Jenny Runacre
Providence – Elaine Stritch

Television
The Avengers – Diana Rigg
The Cilla Black Show
Cleo Laine Special
Two's Company – Elaine Stritch
Dial M for Murder

Sian Phillips wears a design from the hit production of *Pal Joey*, which previewed in the East End in 1980.
John Bates

Choosing a
full stop

10

The Draper's Record, reviewing the John Bates collection for spring 1980, caught the mood for the new decade: 'John Bates's message for eveningwear is draping and slashing to reveal and compliment as much body as possible. Swathed jersey, completely backless and falling in soft folds from the hips. Bates as always knows how to make a girl look like a woman'.

The new decade began with the customary enthusiasm for John Bates designs in the press, from fashion commentators and from customers. The new season's collections were as beautiful and as widely covered as ever, and John went on to dress Sian Phillips in the musical *Pal Joey* to universal acclaim in a 1940s inspired wardrobe. John Swannell created one of the most erotically charged photo shoots ever using John's designs, for the newly opened and extremely fashionable *Ritz* style newspaper, and the sleek, glamorous evening dresses shone from the page. However, 1980 was the year that John chose to close John Bates, and the Jean Varon brand was sold.

Contrary to some reports at the time the businesses were far from bankrupt, but nevertheless the decision was made, twenty-one years after showing the first collection in a flat in Ladbroke Grove. Prudence Glynn in *The Times* reported on 14 October, 'The surprise is the greater because it concerns a fashion house which was regarded within an industry, normally seen as self-indulgent, as particularly sane and well managed.' Jean Muir commented, 'I could have wept. It's such a devastating blow for the industry. What a sombre time. It is getting more and more difficult. You turn your attention away for a minute and things go wrong. Your fabrics are not up to standard, your deliveries are late. Production and quality is a constant headache. All these are strong factors. But it's another brick out of our wall.'

John's clothes had never been more body conscious, erotic, challenging: John Swannell captures the sensuality running through the collections for *Ritz*, the newly opened photography and fashion journal.
John Swannell

John Bates now

As the sun sparkles on the sea, visible from almost every window of the John Bates and John Siggins farmhouse in Wales, the feeling of peace is inescapable. The house sits low in the landscape, surrounded by an immaculate garden; and other than the occasional framed fashion illustration jostling for space on white washed walls with modern British works, there is nothing to give the casual eye any clue as to the meteoric career of one of the most important names in modern British fashion.

Unlike many people who have stepped out of the headlines, John Bates is living and reaping the benefits of the best of his career now, painting, sketching and occasionally designing for private clients. 'I feel as if I'm permanently on holiday', he told Brenda Polan, interviewed for the *Sunday Telegraph* as part of the publicity for his retrospective exhibition at the Fashion Museum in Bath in 2006.

Continued fascination with all things 'Avengers' has been a part of his life since 1965, and often eclipses other aspects of a career which had a greater influence on two decades of British fashion. True to form he faces this with humour and a certain amount of resignation, but he is always ready to talk about them to anyone from American *Vogue* to the *Surrey Advertiser*.

Jean Varon, more than any other label of the 1960s, represented the liberation of fashion from the constraints of couture, making it available to legions of new customers who previously had no access to the latest trends; for this, John Bates should take more kudos than he will ever accept.

He remains a truly unique British talent.

A long way from Ladbroke Grove in 1959: John's studio in Wales today, surrounded by images from *Vogue*.
John Bates

The designer
in person

11

Sian Phillips
Actress

John. Tall, glamorous, talented, kind and generous beyond belief. We first met professionally during rehearsals of *Pal Joey* in 1980. The show began as a fringe production in the East End of London and the budget for my entire wardrobe as a rich Chicago socialite was £200. I don't suppose you could buy a John Bates artificial flower for that. I didn't want to presume on our friendship but I was desperate and I asked John if he would design one of the six costumes; something lovely that I could sing *Bewitched* in. On the spot, he volunteered to design the lot for nothing. I don't think I could have played that part in my first musical without the confidence that came from knowing that I was faultlessly dressed throughout. John dressed me in two other West End shows and the clothes sometimes received their own rounds of applause, which kept me on my toes; one wouldn't want to be upstaged by one's own frock.

I was a private client as well and I have kept all my John Bates dresses, along with a few from Jean Muir, Bill Gibb, Chanel and St. Laurent. The difference is that I actually wear my John Bates, some made specifically for me and many bought off-the-peg. I love extravagantly lovely clothes but I also love them to last, so John's clothes I doubly appreciate.

Fashion can be an acrid business. John is one of that special band of designers who knows how to bring out the best, while concealing the worst features with which his clients are blessed and cursed. We who were lucky enough to be dressed by him felt like Queens; sometimes we even looked like Queens. I miss you John.

The designer at work in Noel Street, late 1970s.
John Bates

162

Gai Pearl
John Bates showroom manager

In the early 1970s I was working as vendeuse and PR at Jean Muir's showroom in Bruton Street but I was soon poached by John Bates and John Siggins to help set up the new John Bates own label line.

Working with them was a pleasure. An atmosphere of good vibrations and humour permeated the business with lots of laughter, jokes, lunches, dinners and Sunday brunches to keep the glossy spirit that was an essential part of the '70s fashion scene alive.

The client list was impressive and one of my most memorable experiences involved an appointment for Princess Alexandra. She was a delightful lady and came in with a briefcase from which she proceeded to extract an enormous Toblerone and an alarm clock which had been set for the time that her chauffeur was to pick her up. During the fitting she asked me if a dress could be made in a different fabric, and in my efforts to please, and aware of the alarm clock ticking, I rushed out to check if this could be done… and after hearing the showroom door click shut realized that I had left the keys behind and I was locked out, and Princess Alexandra was locked in. I rushed into John Siggins's office where he was having a high-powered financial meeting and breathlessly announced 'Help! Quick! The keys! I've locked Princess Alexandra in the showroom!' She never realized… nor did Bates. I think.

I loved John Bates clothes. They were edgier and more dramatic than the softer Missoni or Jean Muir outfits I was used to wearing. John made me my wedding outfit… a jade green wool dress with smocking at the waist and sleeves and a huge sweeping cape and matching hat. I could still wear it now.

Deirdre McSharry
Journalist and former editor of *Cosmopolitan*

On the night in March 1972 that *Cosmopolitan* magazine was launched in the UK I wore a long swirling dress, with tight bodice, sleeves and low neckline in regulation fashion, editor black. (Made from fine wool it was oddly enough redolent of a nun's habit and also had a slyly Puritan look that was a trademark of the designer.)

It was a special from John Bates and had the required effect of making the wearer look taller and more imposing than she – I – was. It must have worked as some months later I was promoted to editor of what had become the most successful woman's magazine in the country.

In the ensuing thirteen or so years as editor of 'Cosmo' I made many calls on John Bates for cover girl dresses – often scarlet – impact clothes for celebrity shoots and personal clothes for special occasions as, looking back, I recall that I seldom left the office to go shopping.

In retrospect it seems that John Bates designs encapsulated the hectic '70s and '80s, when magazine sales were booming, women's lives were busier and more fulfilled, and there was a need for 'notice me' frocks as women were finally making tracks in business, the media and even politics. I recall one young woman MP who cut a brief dash in Labour politics and who owned a Bates frock or two…

In the splendid retrospective show that Rosemary Harden, curator of the Fashion Museum in Bath, staged in the ballroom of The Assembly Rooms in 2006, the impact of the Bates eye for drama – his ability to give even young women stature – was striking. Other than in the rarefied world of couture there were few designers of that period who could deliver clothes with such lavish use of fabric and detail at a price that a young woman in middle management could afford.

Looking through snaps of 'Cosmo' parties the Bates frocks stand out, as the 'Cosmo' staff became more numerous and more confident. In investing in the John Bates label we 'got a lot of bang for our bucks', as we might have phrased it in our mid-Atlantic way in those far-off Seventies.

The essential and adrenalin-fuelled trips to the New York office – the 'Cosmo' mother house – were greatly enhanced by a John Bates little (or long) black dress, glitter pins from Butler and Wilson and a hair up-do by Leonard of Mayfair. Is it too late to thank all three for invaluable ego boosts?

The fact that John Bates was head and shoulders taller than

From the *Sunday Times* archive: a Jean
Varon design from the early 1970s.
Fashion Museum, Bath

most designers – is he not six foot three? – may have given him
that special vision. He can see over the heads of the competition
and certainly saw the impact that the new woman of action, i.e.
Diana Rigg in *The Avengers,* a record-breaking TV series, would
have on the female persona.

I covered the story as woman's editor of *The Daily Express* back
in the Sixties and pictures of Ms Rigg leaping about in tight
leather trousers tailored by John Bates had the same liberating
effect on women's view of themselves as Mick Jagger in his
tight pants had on men. The Avengers collection had the heady
effect on department store sales then that Kate Moss's collection
achieved in 2007.

Images are all important in the world of fashion, and my image
of John Bates, a clever and intuitive designer, a charming host
who threw good parties in his house in Paddington – calm and
white, I recall, with a pretty garden – the ebullient John Siggins,
is of a Nicholas Hilliard miniature (from the time of the first
Queen Elizabeth), the iconic 'Young Man Among Roses', all long
legs, exquisitely cut and embroidered clothes and embowered in
a rambling rose.

Any woman wise enough to have held on to her John Bates
frock has something to hold on to – to treasure – in this day of
disposable fashion. In the meantime you can visit the treasures
in the John Bates Collection at the Fashion Museum, Bath.

Hazel Collins
Model

I remember my first meeting with John Bates as though it were yesterday. I arrived at D'Arblay Street, a narrow tall brick building in London's West End. Above the door was – JOHN BATES – in bold stainless steel letters. I ran up the stairs and rang the door bell. I was ushered in by Gai into a mirrored salon with sumptuous dark chocolate suede couches, sparsely lit by the most enormous stainless steel side table lamps. Gai glided off to find Mr Bates and returned five minutes later.

'Come on in and try a few frocks,' he said. I was petrified but followed him into the dressing room. There were three different garments on the rail. The first dress I put on, gave an illusion that I had grown another foot. The navy blue wool empire line frock hugged the bosom gently. Knee length, the dress grazed the hips elegantly as I moved. Invisible low pockets, inserted into the seam, just below the hip bones, made my hips appear to shrink two inches. And the slightly flared hemline, cut just above the knee, elongated my body further. The dress had full trumpet long sleeves, nipped into a half an inch band fastened by the most exquisite buttons. The length and cut of the sleeves made my arms grow too. When I looked into the mirror my silhouette was transformed into a fashion illustration drawing of pure elegance.

The second was a black wool jersey trouser suit. The short slim line jacket had a high stiff eighteenth century collar, buttoned lapels and padded shoulders with extra long skinny sleeves that finished at the palm of my hand. This was the first tailored jacket I had ever worn. The trousers were impeccably cut, again with invisible low slung pockets. The waist was very high. In fact, the top of the trousers finished just below the ribcage. The craftsmanship was so perfect; I couldn't even find the undetectable zip. These trousers flirted with my bottom and flowed past my feet, so by the time I put on my heels I was effortlessly 6ft plus. The waist was accessorised by the narrowest patent leather belt. The clean outline was gamine and almost androgynous.

The third was the prettiest candy pink silk crepe de chine evening dress. It was a one shoulder gown with a three inch band of the most breathtaking, tightly beaded rhinestones of all sizes across the top of the bosom and over one shoulder. At the top of that shoulder sat an oversized brandy snap twist of rhinestones with two pink six inch tassels dangling either side of the shoulder. Yards of fabric formed the billowing gown. And of course, this robe sported one of the JB insignias – low slung pockets. This garment was glamour and drama – Hollywood style. I felt like the most beautiful woman in the world.

These clothes were so different to anything I had worn. It was the '70s and I was a Quant and Ossie Clarke girl. Youthful and playful garments or romantic silk screened flowing reams of chiffon. John's clothes were architecture at its best, extravagant garments constructed with the most alluring fabrics such as silk crepe de chine, georgette and costly ultra-fine wool mixes – so soft and feminine. The interiors of each garment were so painstakingly moulded that one could wear the dress inside out. There was nothing playful and romantic about John's collection – these frocks were 'grown–up'.

Even the fashion shows, photo calls and magazine shoots were totally different to anything I had done. The fashion shows were held at the Berkeley Hotel ballroom – a large room with pink and grey geometric mirrored wallpaper and carpet to match. The interior design may sound incongruous now, but then, it was so – WOW! Although it was the Seventies and the British economy was pretty grim, champagne and canapés flowed at the Bates extravaganzas.

The models would arrive greeted by John Bates and a glass of champagne. Backstage, it would be hectic – garments being delivered, dressers trying to sort out the frocks on each model's rail. Barbara Daly, the make-up artist, would paint our faces to look like Hollywood's glamorous actresses such as Rita Hayworth and Ava Gardner. The large make-up table top was strewn with every lipstick, blusher and foundation; it looked more like a whole retail make-up counter. Then there was Leonard, the hairdresser, with ten or more stylists and juniors coiffing each head and of course Tony Askew and his production team, along with the lighting and music guys. Some of John Bates's seamstresses would be adding the finishing touches to a few of the garments. The tension would start to build as each model diva started playing up. Their make-up is not quite right, their hair isn't the way they like it. It would be a frenzy of crazed egos.

Suddenly, ten minutes before the show, models' make-up and hair done and ready to go, John Bates would survey each model in their first garment with intent and put his finishing touches. John tied the most perfect bow! Just before the models went onto the runway, John would stick the jewellery on. Cartier, of course!

The front row seats were wall to wall show business glitterati – such as Diana Rigg, Sian Phillips, Peter O'Toole, Joan Collins, David Hemmings, Julie Christie and Maggie Smith, to name a few. Every influential journalist such as B Miller from *Vogue*, Ernestine Carter – the doyenne of fashion, Prudence Glynn (Lady Windlesham) – the first *Times* fashion journalist, Colin

McDowell – the fashion journalist and historian, even the now celebrated Anna Wintour – though a young fashion writer at the time, were poised pen and note books in hand. The atmosphere was pregnant with excitement and anticipation.

As I worked more often with the two Johns, they took me on many trips. We did shows in Paris, Germany and America. But one show in particular stands out in my mind – Paris. I cannot recall what year it was. However, it must have been collection time so most of John's favourite models were working all day in London, and it was not possible to get a commercial flight to Paris.

The Johns simply hired a private plane to take us. The body of the aircraft was so narrow and the ceiling height so low that we had to get down on our hands and knees to crawl into the plane. What is more, when we took off the engine sounded as if it was going to blow up. The whole plane shuddered. We were petrified. Most of us were screaming – including the Johns. It was the shortest but longest trip I have ever had in a private jet.

That night the show was at the British Embassy. The Ambassador and his wife hosted the evening in honour of John. It was a particularly lavish affair. All the French notoriety attended. However, John was not impressed by all this grandeur. He enjoyed hanging out with us, the models observing everyone from afar.

The next day we showed the collection at the imposing Palais de l'Élysée, then on to another show at Versailles. This was a huge hit with the French. But in-between the shows, JB took me with him to his 'French Couture Atelier' where he looked at hundreds of the most intricate exquisite beaded fabrics. Then we went to a sweet shop of buttons. I had never seen such a plethora of the most superb buttons of all sizes, fabrics and metals. Thank goodness our return trip home was on a scheduled commercial flight.

I remember JB's best friend was the Scottish designer Bill Gibb – they attended each other's shows and were true buddies. Together they had a wicked sense of humour and [were] a delight to be around.

I am the proud owner of some of John's pieces that I treasure and still wear, along with the happy memories of those fabulous times.

Barbara Griggs
Author and journalist, former fashion editor of *The Evening Standard* and *Daily Mail*

John Bates was a designer with a gift for the wow-factor. He could do sensational, he could do show-stopping, he could do knockdown dramatic, and he could do outrageous as well as anyone in London or Paris. I still remember the gasp provoked by a beach-dress from 1977 – two handfuls of parma violet silk crepe that slid down the model's body, just covering her breasts, clipped at the waist with a girdle of purple flowers, and disappearing between her legs: it left her sides and thighs bare – but floated out in a charming cape from the shoulders to cover her back. A shocking pink satin monkey-jacket, huge-shouldered, worn with bow-tied white silk shirt, and tightly-waisted black crepe trousers brought the house down at one of his last collections.

In the fashion history books, it's likely to be his eye-catching 'Avengers' range that gets a mention – catsuits, plastic dresses, lots of leather, outfits for judo sessions.

But the thousands of women who bought and wore his dresses over the '60s and '70s are much more likely to remember him for another great quality: how terrific they felt wearing them. Nobody did pretty better than John: in my cuttings-books for the '60s, his trademark empire-line ball-dresses, made in the softest, prettiest prints and fabrics, beribboned and ravishing, leap out from many a page. As his young fans grew up, another great Bates quality matured too: a talent for combining ease with elegance, for skilful cut and structure, for clothes that you could go on wearing and wearing, and which still look good today.

Brigid Keenan
Young Fashion Editor *The Sunday Times* 1962-66, Fashion Editor *The Sunday Times* 1972-75

In 1962 I was working as assistant to the Young Fashion editor at *The Sunday Times* when Fate intervened. My boss, who was pregnant, had to give up her job all of a sudden for health reasons and I was told to carry on with the column as best I could until a replacement could be found. Somehow a replacement never came along and, by default, I became the 'Young Fashion' editor. I always considered myself the luckiest girl on earth.

Very soon in my new career I met John Bates who was working under the label Jean Varon. We were almost the same age – early twenties. He was the nicest, kindest man – as well as enormously talented – visiting his showroom was a treat to look forward to, partly because of the lovely, covetable dresses – but mostly because of the man himself.

The main Fashion Editor of *The Sunday Times* at that time was the formidable Ernestine Carter. I dragged her to meet John and she became as smitten as every other fashion writer was. *The Sunday Times* often featured his clothes – either on Ernestine's page, or mine (I remember doing a story on his wardrobe for Diana Rigg in *The Avengers,* and something on his string vest dresses called, oh dear, 'Go Vest Young Woman'), and later, when the colour magazine came into existence, on Meriel McCooey's lovely lively pages.

Now John's clothes have become museum pieces (how I regret not keeping mine; where did they go? How do clothes simply disappear out of your wardrobe?) But better than any dresses are my memories of hilarious, happy times spent with John Bates.

The longer, sophisticated look of the early 1970s, with a hint of Edwardian elegance.
Fashion Museum, Bath

Rosemary Harden
Curator, Fashion Museum, Bath

A curator's work is all about collections of original material. It's also about coming up with ways of presenting and making sure that people know about these collections, that they can see them, learn from them, be inspired by them, and enjoy them.

Back in April 2003 I received an email addressed to the Curator of the then Museum of Costume with photographs of a red velvet dress by Jean Varon. The sender added that he would love to donate the dress to the museum, adding in brackets 'if you want it!'

It has to be said that pieces that are offered to the Fashion Museum (which is based in the Assembly Rooms in Bath) frequently duplicate one of the 60,000 plus objects already in the museum collection, and we therefore regularly decline offers of donations. However, in this instance, the unassuming little 'if you want it!' struck an immediate chord. There was no question whether I would want it; curatorially speaking I would have crossed continents for it!

The work of John Bates for Jean Varon in the 1960s and 1970s had long been a personal passion. In a previous job I had once let a red wool Jean Varon dress from the early 1970s slip through my hands by failing to accept it for that particular museum's collection. I knew almost immediately that I had made the wrong decision. The decision (whilst not quite haunting me) remained with me until I had worked for a little while in my present job. One day, I discovered that the very same red wool dress had ended up in the collection at Bath. Was it by chance, or could it be kismet?

After I had been at Bath a little longer I discovered too that John Bates and John Siggins were great supporters of the Museum. They had visited on a number of occasions and had generously donated fashions made under the John Bates label (which was described at the time as 'almost ready-to-wear clothes'). It was an important donation, with added value because there were connections too with the Museum's extensive collection of black and white photographs, known as 'The Sunday Times Fashion Archive'. This collection, from the late 1950s to the early 1960s included images (a number of which are reproduced in this book) of John's work, both for Jean Varon and his other labels.

Back now to that email from 2003. The writer was Richard Lester and my reply was an emphatic 'yes please'. The red velvet dress was subsequently accessioned to the collection, becoming BATMC 2003.43, and the donation was the beginning of a warm and continuing association between Richard and the Fashion Museum. In 2004 he donated his entire holding of the designer to the Museum and, up to the time of writing, the John Bates Collection is way past the 500 garment mark.

What happens to the John Bates garments when they arrive at the Fashion Museum? At the risk of sounding mundane, curatorial work is also about collection accountability, a sort of specialised stock control (making sure we know what there is in the collection, and where it is located at any time). The Fashion Museum Collection assistant undertakes a meticulous object entry process (day book, accession book, gift form, thank you letter, collection inventory, donor's file, accession number) for every dress which is intended to become part of the Museum collection. The final challenge is to find space to store all these 500 plus dresses on the Museum site. This is no small feat in the Museum storage area, which, by repute, used to be the flat where the caretaker of the Assembly Rooms lived. But every dress is carefully stored on padded coat hangers made by the Fashion Museum's volunteer team especially for the John Bates dresses.

At the back of my mind I always had the idea that we should use the donation as an opportunity to put on a major fashion exhibition in Bath showcasing John's work as there had never been a museum retrospective devoted solely to him. I felt amongst the Museum visitors, those in the know would enjoy reliving their youth and those who weren't (probably the majority of the visitors) would enjoy finding out about the work of one of the unsung heroes of British fashion.

Eventually the exhibition *John Bates: Fashion Designer* went on show at the Museum in the summer of 2006, after a gestation period of over two years. We worked closely with John Bates, John Siggins and with Richard Lester to create a display featuring over 80 examples of John's work. The exhibition was organised in a series of nine broadly chronological themes from the Empire line and the Sixties to the John Bates label of the mid and late 1970s. It was immensely popular with visitors of all ages enjoying the startling sight of so many dresses and such varied fashions, all displayed on original Rootstein mannequins.

What next for the John Bates Collection at the Museum? There is work to be done to discover and to record fuller catalogue information about each of the pieces – for example we are not sure of the exact date of some of the garments, which collections they were from, where they retailed and for how much. It would be good to find out more about the design story, the manufacturing process, the marketing histories, as well as who wore them, why, where and how they felt.

We know that key pieces from John's career at Jean Varon are not yet part of the Fashion Museum Collection. It would be excellent, for example, to be able to acquire for the collection one of the floral shift dresses complete with matching stockings from 1964, or a bra dress, or indeed some of *The Avengers* pieces from 1965. The John Bates Collection must be one of the largest collections of garments by one fashion designer in any museum in the UK. We plan to both expand the collection, and to continue to seek ways to make sure that people can learn from, be inspired by and enjoy the work of John Bates.

Felicity Green
Journalist, Senior Lecturer in Fashion Journalism at St Martin's School of Art, elected to the Press Gazette Hall of Fame in 2005

He was tall, he was handsome. He had a sophisticated sardonic manner and to tell the truth I was always a little afraid of him. Perhaps this was because he mostly made clothes for tall elegant women and I wasn't tall! But when you were with him talking fashion he had a great sense of humour and his clothes reflected this. He made clothes for youthful fun and games but his handwriting included some of the most beautiful best-of-the-ball evening dresses that combined theatre with glamour. He managed this with astute appreciation of the changing times and the impact of swinging London on the whole fashion scene; his repertoire cleverly included lots of gingham and colourful gaiety for the youth of the day plus some very sophisticated numbers for the ladies who lunched.

I remember walking through Harrods one day with Digby Morton, a famous British couturier. We spied a famous six feet tall lady who lunched, clad top to toe in the svelte Bates style of the times. To complete the narrow slinky silhouette she had added a large ascot type hat. 'Goodness me,' said Digby, 'what an elegant standard lamp!'

John's innate sense of fun made him perfect for the newly bold generation who craved impact more than understated style. I featured one such dress in the *Daily Mirror* at that time. The headline called it 'The Smallest Dress in the World'. And it justified the claim. The bra top comprised a few strategically placed leaves and the gap between the top and the brief bottom made it less of a dress and more of a two piece apology. But it apparently sold well at 10 and a half guineas which worked out at a penny farthing a square inch.

Today John is a successful artist and his paintings tell their own story of a man of style with an eye for beauty that still flourishes. Beauty of beauty.

Opposite page
A typical Jean Varon publicity shot from the mid-1970s, photographed on house model 'Titch' and distributed to the press by John Siggins.
John Bates

Index

With thanks to: John Bates and John Siggins, whose humour, hospitality and total cooperation made writing a pleasure; Mark Eastment, Matthew Freedman and all at ACC for backing the book; Marit Allen, Sian Phillips, Barbara Griggs, Felicity Green, Brigid Keenan, Deirdre McSharry, Hazel Collins, Gai Pearl and Sue Jarrett for their sparkling text; Sinty Stemp, Meriel McCooey, John Swannell, Ralf Nodder, Danielle and the Condé Nast team, *The Sunday Times,* IPC Magazines and National Magazines for assistance with images; Rosemary Harden, Howard Batho and the Fashion Museum in Bath for the John Bates retrospective in 2006; Robert Shaw and the Northbank designers; and Geoff Cox, whose encouragement started the ball rolling.